I0125830

Marcenus Rodolphus Kilpatrick Wright

The mastereon

Reason and recompense, a revelation concerning the laws of mind

Marcenus Rodolphus Kilpatrick Wright

The mastereon
Reason and recompense, a revelation concerning the laws of mind

ISBN/EAN: 9783337120467

Printed in Europe, USA, Canada, Australia, Japan

Cover: Foto ©Suzi / pixelio.de

More available books at **www.hansebooks.com**

THE
MASTEREON,

OR

REASON AND RECOMPENSE,

A

REVELATION

CONCERNING THE

Laws of Mind

AND

Modern Mysterious Phenomena,

BY

MARCENUS R. K. WRIGHT

THE SELF-MADE AUTHOR AND SEER.

———— ··

CHICAGO,
RELIGIO-PHILOSOPHICAL PUBLISHING HOUSE
S. S. JONES & CO.,
1872.

DEDICATION.

To those who seek for knowledge, who love reflection, who enjoy freedom of thought, are unbiassed in mind and unprejudiced in purpose, who are fully released from the trammels of a conformable intellectuality and all associative circumscription in life; to those who are ministers of their own mentality and hold to a studied consistency in all dealing, who are willing to acknowledge the truth without self-abuse of conscience and who labor for the general good of man, this, the first volume of the "Mastereon," is most respectfully dedicated by

THE AUTHOR.

CONTENTS.

Introductory Preface.

The preface to a book is as necessary to its composition, as the gilt-edged frame of a looking-glass is needful to its ornamentation and finish. It is the mirror wherein is reflected the design of the author. His objects, whether good or bad, are indicated in its words; and the subjects whereof he treats are foreshadowed in that "light of wisdom" which he alone possesses, and which is the measure of his qualification, ability or success.

The present volume was written with the intention of explaining a mystery—the mystery of the action of the mental faculties in their more interior and abnormal exercise. The writer is himself a subject of *abseneistic* entrancement of mind, and has suffered the severest trials and punishments, as well as enjoyed the fullest happiness which man is capable of experiencing at the hands of "invisible powers" under the influence of psychology.

Personally I hold to no man's opinions, and accept only those conclusions which are supported by inferences well founded in reason, or which are based upon those essential details of knowledge which science can fully recognize and adopt as true. The idealisms and fictitious sentimentality of either the opponents or advocates of certain existing, and some-

what popular theories, it is not my purpose to regard
or consider; while to trim and fashion my individual
thoughts to conform to the standard measure of any
system of religion, any pattern of philosophy, or the
expectations of those who career their "spiritual
aptisms" before the world, on the ground of their
origin in the wisdom of the "saints of heaven," is
an object wholly at varience with the established
convictions and fixed purpose of my understanding.

An experience of better than three years continuance as a subject of conversational communion
with "invisible beings," and visioned observation
of the conditions of life which they inherit, necessarily induces and supports a belief in the author's
mind, that all systems of religion which have been
founded and sustained by men and governments
during past ages, or which belong to a more recent
period, are but the result of eclesiastical solicitude,
or circumstances connected with the advancement
and progress of mankind, and cannot be said to be a
manifestation of that exalted and quiet wisdom which
is never flattered, and which supplies its shafts of in-
telectual light to restrain rather than cajole or excite
human belief and confidence.

The claim which I herein advance to an artic-
ulate hearing "in the spirit," or to audable converse
with the immortals *in the mind*, is susceptable of the
clearest and most satisfactory demonstration, not
only as a question of practical interest with spirits,
but one which science may easily reach through the
law of analogy, and establish over all objections, or
attempts at confutation.

At first thought it may appear to some that this singular, silent process of communion with the departed, is a privilege much to be enjoyed, and one which could bring only peace, contentment and satisfaction to the soul. But this is not so. In truth, so far as individual happiness is concerned, positive personal experience in almost every instance clearly substantiates an exactly opposite conclusion. For as between the practical righteousness and purposed mischief of spirits, and the doubts, quibbles and misgivings of men, the clairvoyant receives but little enjoyment or consolation in the interblended life, which it is his to accept at the hand of his invisible guardian.

The communion of spirits with mortals, and the somnambulic life of the seer, are questions which involve the most serious reflection, as a consequence of the mystery in which they have been enwrapt; and even those of whom, most of all, it would seem that we might expect more lucid and consistent explanations, are in reality themselves but too often deceived or misled in understanding, owing to self-assumption, credulity, pride, haste or indifference, and are therefore but ill-qualified to satisfy or exalt the human mind by a truthful or accordant revelation of facts and secrets, which are thus suspended in uncertainty and the analysis of critical argumentation.

Selfish motives and arrogance, it is true, are many times a source of success, where genuine mental worth, and ability humbly given, are humiliated by defeat. The most wondrous schemes, involving good as well as evil purposes, are usually concocted in the darkest closets. Thus, while it may be of interest at times, for the mind to withhold its knowledge from common observation and comment, as a means of self-protection and as a choice in the peaceful persuit of life; still it cannot be said to be just or wise for men or spirits to exercise thought in deceitful conceal-ment of truth, or needful to barter away a worthy judgment for those literary riddles, which veil and mystify the plain suggestions of reason and common sense.

In dealing with all phenomena it should become the just and considerate purpose of the human mind to concede a propriety in liberal and consistent criti-cism, and this sentiment should be rendered practical in the exercise of thought, as well as material to the production of all literature which pertains to religion, science or philosophy. Our safety in belief is only to be secured by strict adherence to caution, hesi-tancy and delay, in the acceptance of new ideas and opinions. Credulity is, indeed, the last concession which man should consider acceptable, and it were even better to parry the presence of truth for a while, than to become the subject of unwise haste in matters of thought, sentimentality or confidence.

The author holds to nature as the source of life, and accepts the evidence of a Divine Presence and Infinite Guardianship as inseperably associated there-with. Nature is to him the "all in all" of destiny, of existence, the "only hope" of mind, the basis of all expectation or certainty in being, and the only promise ever given to man of a life of eternal con-tinuance and progress.

All life is founded *in* nature, is *of* nature, and *from* nature can never be *released*. Man is clothed with an outer vesture, and dwells upon the surface of a terrestrial sphere, receiving his sustenance and support from the various products of nature which surrounds him. The spirit, being released from its external barriers, lives within the confines of the aerial heavens, a *wa-de-un* or immersed condition of existence, and is supported by *ethereal respiration*.

The ostensable object held in view in publishing a series of articles to be embodied in volumes under the general title of the "Mastercon," is to teach the "philosophy of life," to explain the motives represented in the "principle of justice," as viewed in the light of its appointments and application to the needs of objects and things in the temple of nature, and to the interests of the human mind. There are two extremes of manifestation alternating and co-operating in the universe to the inevitable production of Power and Purpose, and it is quite evident that the "golden mein" is the "poise of wisdom" around which the unstaid and ever-persistent energies and activities evolved in creation, move with steadfast consistency and unyielding force, to the ultimate and constant production of innumerable, diversified, fixed and moving forms.

The evolution of thought in organic periphery of vital and self-conscious life, is nature's greatest success, and when once established, the *mind* forever prompts its own advantage in being, through the amplification of a genius secured in contention, opposition. and the never-ceasing struggle for self-satis-

faction in existence. It is designed to consider the
"philosophy of immortality," and to substantiate the
impartial and unselfish design of the Infinite, All-
providing Spirit, in his bestowment of eternal life
upon all mankind alike. It is also designed to reflect upon the important and deeply interesting subject of "futurity," the relation which we at present
sustain to *interior* and more exalted realms of being,
and the cause of the unhappy demonstrations and
mystery, with which the "invisibles" are many times
wont to clothe their acts and manifestations, in their
dealing and intercourse with mankind.

In treating of these and kindred themes of thought
we are likely to differ with many thinkers and stu-
dents in philosophy, with many writers upon metaphysical subjects, and those seers of the past and
present, who have chosen to adopt theories, or advance conclusions, as based altogether upon the advice
of spirits and that abnormal state so peculiar to their
mental experience. The condition of the unseen inhabitants of higher spheres is a question not yet
answered to the entire satisfaction of the human
mind, and the appearance of spirit beings, as seen in
the deepest visions of clairvoyance, may in a degree
be reflected upon as a mission in *concealment of the
actual* when the history of phenomena and the science
of optics is wisely regarded.

Spiritualism in its phenomenal aspect is phenom-
enally unchanged in all the ages, and is permanent
in its obligation or fidelity, to a system of enigmati-
cal and untrustworthy developments—manifestations
which annoy and perplex the intellect, which confuse

the understanding, and trifle with the heart in its anxiety and sincere search after a knowledge of the conditions of trans-mundane existence.

It will appear evident to those who see fit to peruse the contents of this volume, and more especially to those who are familiar with the principles of psychology and the entranced action of man's mental faculties, that the privilege which I herein affirm to possess as a "natural clairvoyant," as well as the singular method of confirmation by which it was established, is as truly wondrous in its more unhappy features, as it is remarkable as an extraordinary accomplishment in a somnambulic transition of mind.

While I regard it as the greatest pleasure which I am ever likely to enjoy as a dweller in outward life, to speak in conversational familiarity with the spirit kindred of my Father's Household, and others wherein it is permitted, I at the same time deem it needful to conform to the strictest and most rigid rules of reason in my dealings with and receipt of intelligence from them; and I would in every case admonish zealots and enthusiasts, to restrain their anxiety, and avoid that patrimony of the "future life," which is too frequently conceived in uneasiness, haste and folly.

Mind may properly serve itself only in the more quiet and desirable ways of wisdom. The peace and happiness of the world is more or less interfered with, by our solicitous attention to those subjects which are deeply veiled in the ample folds of the mantle of nature. Under the almost insensible in-

XIV INTRODUCTORY PREFACE.

fluence of psychology, as practiced by the missionary monitors of the inward realms of life, the mind is often deceived in regard to the cause of its own decisions, and feels a responsibility on account of its duties and operations which in truth should rest with the discretion, goodness, or otherwise ill-chosen intentions of unseen and intelligent beings.

Could the author have foreknown the extent of his trials and sufferings, or the effect of spirit-magnetization upon his mental faculties, he would have early restrained his feelings of anxiety and desire, as occasioned by his love for and hope in an immortal existence, and would certainly have shunned, rather than have accepted the decision of a spirit-brother in his behalf, as a mesmeric subject of his will.

The human mind is in reality but an organic instrument, singularly acute in its sensibilities, and may be played upon by invisible beings or agents, with the same ease and precision with which a good musician is enabled to play or execute music upon his favorite piano or violin. The unseen, aerial magnetizer may cause his subject to remember or forget, to feel active or stupid, wakeful or sleepy, ugly and snarling or joyous and pleasant, may revive old memories, lead the person into misery, prompt unwise desires, inflame the passions, or point the way to happiness, success and worthy expectation in life.

Mankind will ere long discover that man is as nature intended him to be, both as to the good and ill results presented in the characteristics and manifestations of his being, and that the most wondrous

law associated with his existence and destiny is the
law of PSYCHOLOGY, which, when rightly understood,
or properly comprehended, will constitute a most
marvelous revelation of the wisdom of the Omnipotent
mind, as displayed in the spiritual interests of the
boundless universe, over which he casts his merciful
influence and wields supreme command.

I claim no infallibility as a seer, and believe in
none as pertaining to those who have lived in former
ages. While it is true that the clairvoyant is a subject of the most sensitive mind, and may receive
absolute knowledge concerning many things which
are hidden from ordinary inspection, it is also quite
as certain that the very sensitiveness of his nature
is a basis for the unconscious committal of frequent
mistakes and blunders, if not of acts more objectionable, as founded in the mesmeric control of the immortals.

The story of the author's somnambulic career, or
a goodly portion thereof, is hereby introduced, that
the reader may have the benefit of a more extended
acquaintance with the facts and circumstances which
have tended to produce his most singular mental
realizations. Although it might seem desirable, it is
deemed impracticable at the present time to give a
fuller explanation. It is hoped however that in the
future, and at no very distant day, a more complete
statement may be presented, one which shall embody
every shade of thought which may have a bearing
upon the subject of a personal experience in many
particulars, quite as marvelous, as its lessons are
likely to be, to most minds, inscrutable.

Three years and a half have now elapsed since I first listened to the speech of spirits. During that entire period I have passed no day without conversations with my angel guardian, spirit kindred and friends. My brother, who is my watchful protector, and guide lives above my head somewhere within the limit of the atmosphere. He speaks with me as kindly, though not as familiarly as when upon the earth previous to his desease, which occurred when I was a boy, some twenty-seven years ago. When he first revealed himself to me, in the winter of 1868, I was in every way an incompetent scholar. By his aid I have so far advanced in a knowledge of letters as to be able, not only to write very well, but to read, correct and punctuate my own compositions. I have no knowledge, only that derived from conversations and visions, concerning the position of my Brother in the atmosphere. His life is greatly changed. I am not prepared to speak as to this matter in any particular sense in this volume. I am satisfied that many of the ideas of spiritualists concerning the departed are as fictitious as the arts and wiles of misery itself. My Brother appears to love me as fondly as when a denizen in outward life. But there is a *law of mystery* dominating over *sincerity* in the spirit world, which prevents the consumation of desirable happiness in communion, as between them and us. The little which I receive from my brother and others in spirit is meeted out to me under restraints and the bickerings of this law—a condition of things, which however wise as in the interest of the "superior life," I could not personally approve in the light of *my* knowledge of the principles of goodness, justice, truth and righteousness.

That spirits are more wise than mortals can conceive is a truth which may ere long be learned through sad experience. All the opposition of men is futile as against the psychologic power pushed in the interest of our progress by unseen beings. The Angels of Wisdom ride the aereal stratifications above us to qualify every judgment of man, wherein there is abuse of human life. Theology is the score which mortals may settle by the aid of the Angel World. Let us hope that our differences may be adjusted without incurring penalties which would malign our good sense, or destroy our hopes in that heaven to which we are all tending in spite of our opinions.

With these prefatory and somewhat extended explanations and considerations the reader is referred to the semi-biographical and critical narrative which constitutes this the first valume of the "Mastereon."

The Mastereon.

CHAPTER I.

THE ABSENEIST. INITIAL REFLECTIONS.

In considering the highest form of psychological development, a condition of mind known to scientists as clairvoyance, and which in its ultimate stretch of power, of vision, of knowledge, is as really true as it is marvelous, we are obliged to conform in our reasonings and conclusions, to that privilege of personal experience and education which limits all individual ability, yet which furnishes the only reliable evidence upon which to found a practical judgment.

Somnambulism is a peculiar form of mental manifestation, and its more negative phases are ever prophetic of an exaltation of the senses in interior light and knowledge. When once attained this condition of mind is both a source of personal success and happiness. Many are the mistaken claims to the prerogatives of intelligence which it confers, and terrible is the degradation to which the word clairvoyant has been subjected.

If persons by any influence become subject to involuntary movements of the arm, or feel the impulse of magnetic forces acting upon the nervous system, they at once begin to pride themselves upon their ability as Clairvoyants. The supercilious physician, looking to the interests involved in the pursuit of his daily practice, puts the hoodwink of Clairvoyance over the eyes of the public, and covering his falsifications too deep for ordinary inspection or discernment, secures his individual credit, while arrogating to himself the propriety of practicing a "yankee trick," or of making life conform to the "art of duplicity."

Thousands of persons imbued with incipient psychologic impulses, as imposed upon them from invisible sources, have felt an occasional and unexpected inclination to involuntary muscular movements, while others have become unconsciously entranced through the force of will, as exercised by a guardian missionary of the inner life. But to win that worthy attainment in knowledge and understanding, which enables the mind to look upon the scenes of the invisible, and converse with the immortals in audible speech of the Spirit, is to reach a condition of optical and auditory permissions as little understood as they are rarely attained.

Mind is abased by assumption, as it is elevated by strict obedience to straight-forward consistency. Hence it should be our uniform desire to speak with

candor, when asking the confidence of men to our
claims as possessors of any new or unusual phase
of mental development, whether naturally or phe-
nomenally exhibited, for by so doing we avoid the
derision of our own honor, and retain the respect
and esteem of others in the privilege which we enjoy.

The *actual* in clairvoyant experience, as produced
by unseen agents, is still deeply hidden from the
comprehension of men, more perhaps as a consequence
of the impracticability of a free disclosure, than from
a want of *media* or channels through which to obtain
it; and notwithstanding the many efforts of scientists
to fathom the mysteries of mind as abnormally presented, the whole subject still remains overshadowed
by doubts, uncertainties and qualifications, which time
and honest investigation alone may prove adequate
to remove.

One of the most singular features presented in
connection with all psychologic manifestations is to
be found in the utter want of perspicuity which is
displayed in their examination. Investigators have
engaged in the study of this science with greater
curiosity of mind, than serenity or sincerity of purpose, and owing to the difficulty of readily reaching
an understanding of the cause of mental action, and
more especially in its abnormal features, they have
either abandoned the subject altogether in haste, believing it to be to profound for research or comprehension, or under the ban of popular fears and objections, have advanced a score of visionary theories,
alike destructive of the interests of truth, as they
are confusing to the student of mental philosophy.

Those who have claimed to enjoy the highest privilege in *absenteeism* of mind, have conferred upon themselves but little credit for the lucidity of their interpretation of mental or metaphysical phenomena, and while claiming to possess a permission in the exercise of dual intellectual powers, either from motives in self-regard or from *interior* psychologic debarment, they have reserved their knowledge from public keeping.

Mind may be ever so familiar with the "invisibles," may converse by "impressional thought" in all the perfection of distinct articulation, it may seem to wander through the heavens in the enjoyment of clairvoyant visions and return to the outward sense with unfledged memory, but the consciousness of the actual possession of *spirit sight* as disconnected with the material substance of the natural eye—the retina and its brain connections—is in no mortal man to be made valid as a claim; neither is it possible to establish the practicability of such disembodyment of life, in view of the present advanced condition of optical science, and those who demand concessions to a claim so improbable, are either themselves honestly mistaken in regard to the manner of the production of visions, or knowing the cause and manner of their development are guilty of the practice of a species of *candid duplicity* in presuming to withhold from the public a proper knowledge of most important facts.

Clairvoyance is the slippery ground which lies between full consciousness as in outward life, and the silence of a super-terrestrial realm of existance. It is

the "deep sleep" wherein the mental faculties are
calm and free to be *acted upon*, or impressed with
inward realizations by spirit magnetizers, *in a sense
in consonance with the natural action of the mind.*

Visions are objectively and subjectively a mesmeric
production, and are always under the direction of an
operator.   All images and scenes thus presented are
forced upon the faculties of perception by the action
of a foreign will, and it is a fiction to suppose that
a condition of self-induced trance is possible, or that
any state of trance in which intelligence is manifested,
may be developed without aid from extraneous sources.

Mind cannot be released from its association with
the nervous fiber or cell substance of the brain until
physical dissolution absolutely occurs, and although
visions may be granted to the clairvoyant embodying
all the wondrous beauty and perfection of stereoscopic pictures, still these scenes so gorgeous and grand,
so indiscribably perfect, are visions only *in the mind*,
enstamped thereon by beings who hold the particulars of the scene in their own conception, and impart the counterthought or reflection thereof—so to
speak—to the subject's mind by the power of will.
Hence, visions are not the result of observation
through the eyes of the spirit, as freed from its
association with the constituent elements of the outward eye and brain, but are pictures hung upon the
walls of the mind by spirit desire, to be gazed upon
in the stillness and death-like condition of trance, or
magnetic slumber.

We cannot go beyond the bound of mental action
as associated with brain substance, for a solution

of the problem of *interior* sight. Mind rests within its enfolded limits, and all its manifestations and re-alizations are confined within the barriers fixed in the organic relation of the chemical compounds of the material form.

It is manifest evidence of short-sightedness in arriving at logical conclusions, to suppose that the spirit may be released from its connection with the physical body in clairvoyance, or even that such dis-union of soul and body is necessary to the attainment of its most exalted condition. When mind is locked up in the "deep sleep" of somnambulistic abstraction, it is living in abeyance of another's desires and will, and is in reality only an instrument, well or ill attuned to the purpose of the reception of visions or intelligence, as placed to the account of its faculties by "ministering spirits," who possess a full and prac-tical knowledge of all its powers, capacities and capabilities.

We are not willing to assert that those who enter the state of clairvoyance are at all times re-sponsible for the mistakes which they commit, either as regards the details of statements which they pre-sent, or the disclosures which they offer for public consideration while in that condition, from the fact that the *subjugation* of mind in psychology presupposes irresponsibility. But when the mental faculties are unencumbered and free from all *imposed* influences, then the individual should regard his or her experi-ence in the light of external reason, and endeavor to determine how much, and how far such interior de-velopment of mind should be allowed to govern life's

outward interests, and should never willingly permit
credence or enthusiasm to precede the exercise of dis-
crimination and judgment.

As mortals we may *have*, and memory may *cherish* the most singular fancies and realizations, but it
is only when we arrive at manhood's or womanhood's
maturer years, that we are enabled to properly consider the usefulness of all the circumstances and incidents which have, or may come within the sphere
of our observation, or which have fallen to our lot
as individuals, and make them guides to personal improvement and education.

The science of psychology is best known as a
science of mental influences, developed by mesmeric
control under the action of an operator.   Its results
are produced by the positive and negative relations
established between mind and mind through desire or
mutual purpose and effort.

In the absence of reliable knowledge concerning
the future life and spirit ability, mankind have mostly
attributed such phenomena, especially when occurring
in the form of "possession," "obsession," or "witchcraft," to demoniacal presence, to desease, insanity
and hallucination, instead of finding the real and responsible cause, through earnest research and investigation.

Upon our knowledge of existence depends our
success in being.   In view of this fact and wishing
for the best good of every person living, we now
solicit the companionship and confidence of the reader,
while we journey along the rugged and mysterious
pathway of abseneistic thought and experience, reach-

ing from childhood through better than thirty years of life; and in the pursuit of our object we hope and pray that we may be enabled to serve a worthy purpose in explaining some of the most difficult problems involved in mental science and spiritual philosophy,

---

CHAPTER II.

EARLY RECOLLECTIONS, VISIONS AND THOUGHTS.

When I was a small boy, being only three years old, I was one day with my mother in the cellar of our large house where she had gone for the purpose of obtaining some provisions for the family table, when being in that semi-somnambulic condition of mind which is quite natural to me, and looking about, I distinctly saw the shadowy figure of a child accompanied by a large black dog or animal, which she was leading in the direction of the open doorway through which we had but just entered the underground apartment. In the excitement and anxiety which the apparition occasioned in my mind, and at

the very moment I observed its appearance, I said to
her in whom I then placed my trust and confidence
as a child: "Oh! mother, what is that strange thing
walking across the cellar," when under the influence
of fear I clung to her side in the fullness of my
desire for safety.

My mother seeing no propriety in my conduct,
and wondering at what she considered a very singular "freak of fancy," as represented in my statements
and actions, very seriously remarked, "don't be so
foolish, my boy, there's nothing in the cellar to hurt
you," when fulfilling the domestic mission which she
had in view, she took me by the hand and led me
out into the yard behind the house, and thence into
the kitchen, where I soon found employment for my
thoughts as well as ultimate relief from the memory
of my vision.

This little incident occurring, as it did, at that
early period of my life, was necessarily as new and
strange to me, as it was unaccountable and unpleasant, and, although it left a deep and lasting impression upon my youthful mind, it did not at that time
seem to foreshadow any particular event, or have
any special signification. But we are naturally led
to inquire as a result of the appearance of such an
apparition: What were the more minute peculiarities
represented in its movements? How long did it
remain visible? What was the probable cause of its
production? Was the vision desirable? Did the
objects seen appear to hold a real and tangible
identity, or did they embody merely vaporish and
unsubstantial characteristics?

Mind naturally looks to *itself* for a solution of the mysteries which pertain to its existence. It wanders in search of the intangible and the uncertain, through a love for the *idea* or hope of immortality, and a desire for a knowledge of its truth, and of the cause, if any there be, of its unrestricted continuance in individualized consciousness and self-poised identity; and in its reasonings concerning the ideal and the invisible, it ever bases its conclusions upon the best evidence at its command. In regarding all mental phenomena therefore, and especially that which seems to have no adequate cause, it becomes needful to make candid inquiry in relation to every attendant fact and circumstance, before rendering a final judgment as to its purport, merit, reality, value or object. We should inquire why a child should be able to see a thing which did not and could not exist as a genuine reality. Why a grown person in the same apartment should be unable to discover any object, and why the apparition itself should appear and disappear in such precise and unlooked for order, the mind being unable to duplicate itself in disagreeable illusions or develope within itself systematic scenes wholly at variance with its inclinations and thoughts. These are questions which will bear reflection, and which, while they may prove to be somewhat difficult to answer, are sure to become a source of pleasure as well as of instruction to the intellect, when once understood or properly comprehended.

The singularity of all interior events and their signification can best be known when the mind is well unfolded in its capacity to discern the relation which we hold as sentient beings to a higher life, and that inscrutable, will-engendered power which is exercised over us by unseen agents, or, in other words, when we are able to fathom the relation which inward causative action sustains to outward appearances, movements and manifestations. If those who earnestly seek for a knowledge of the more hidden and mysterious secrets pertaining to philosophy, metaphysics and the realms of the immortal, would but assume the responsibility of fearless investigation, thus making themselves acquainted and familiar with the essential circumstances and conditions which tend to veil our perceptions and annoy as well as confound reason in its effort to rise in enlightment and wisdom, they would unquestionably soon discover that all so called "unaccountable developments" and "marvelous manifestations," whether of a physical or mental nature, are susceptable of receiving a rational and satisfactory explanation.

It is uniformly the custom with bigots and superficialists to ignore the *actuality* of the strange and varied occurrances, which here and there, now and then, attract so much of public attention, and to condemn all phenomena which are accredited to invisible and intelligent causes; and but few are willing to admit that any "practical good" is likely to be derived from an understanding of those psychologic or mental influences, which ever have, and still continue to interblend all human experience with a solemn element of mystery.

When I was somewhat older, and upon an occasion when least expected, it was again my privilege to observe the same strange figures as they passed before me, crossing the roadway along which I was walking in the night time, toward our family residence. A little child which seemed to be not more than five years old, appeared upon the path at some distance in front of my position, seeming to come through an opening or gateway which led into a broad yard to my left. As she passed along without seeming to observe anything, I noticed the same large dark colored animal following close behind her, which I had seen upon the former occasion, when in the cellar with my mother, some five years previous. They moved slowly across the broad road to the right of my position, and as they approached an old stone building, on the opposite side from where I stood, very suddenly disappeared from my view. Under the impulse of a very unpleasant feeling—a sense of fear and anxiety resulting from what I had seen—I said to my Brother who was with me, and who was some seven years older than myself, and evidently unconscious of what had presented itself to my vision. "Oh! Jacob"—for that was his name— "did you see that little girl and great big dog going across the road just now."

"No," said he, "don't be so foolish, my eyes are as good as yours I guess; hav'nt seen anything." When, noticing that I was frightened and that I clung to his side for safety, he took me by the hand and again remarked: "Come now, you're a simpleton, you're certainly mistaken, for I hav'nt seen a single thing, and I don't believe you have."

"Yes I have," I replied, somewhat mortified at

being doubted in regard to my honest and unselfish statements, "I never was more certain of anything in all my life, but you needn't believe it unless you choose."

Brother laughed to hear me sputter, and said: "I guess when you get home and get to bed you'll think no more about spooks and apparitions."

Notwithstanding my Brother was unwilling to admit that I had seen anything, still in my own mind I was well satisfied that I had, and for some unaccountable reason I could not avoid conforming to the inclination of my mind, which seemed fixed in reflection upon the subject.

As we passed along the pathway leading toward home, it being quite dark--the moon having suddenly disappeared behind a dense mass of clouds which arose from the west—and also late at night, I clung more closely to his side, through childish timidity and fear, until we reached the very door which opened into the kitchen of our old house, when feeling my courage revive and return with unusual force, and conceiving that my sincere confidence and honesty had been questioned, I very crustily remarked, in reply to some taunting expression which he had used in regard to my ghost-seeing proclivities, that, "if he'd mind his own affairs I'd thank him very much."

We had now entered the family sitting room, and no sooner was Brother seated, then with a mischievous and mirthful look he commenced to relate to those present the story of my vision, peculiar actions and fears, equally to the derision of my plea-

sure and the excitation of their joy and delight.
Thinking that silence was commendable, or realizing
that contention was useless and unavailing, I soon
left the jocose party, who were having a laugh at
my expense, and with a short and surly "I don't
care; perhaps some of you'll see something that'll
trouble you some time," I retired to the chamber
where I usually slept, and crawling into bed all
alone, was soon lost to every outward sense of consciousness or infelicity.

Arising early on the subsequent morning, I
thought but little of the affair of the previous night,
and only as I was occasionally reminded of it by my
Brother and Father, who loved to see me annoyed
by their questionings and intimations concerning it,
did I ever speak of this most singular and twice
repeated scene of my early life, and consequently it
was only treasured in the deep depths of my memory to be reflected upon or regarded in after time as
a curious incident, not unlike many others which
frequently occur as a result of abseneistic abstraction
of mind.

It is well known to those who are acquainted
with the laws of psychology and mental control, that
any operator may impose objective·visions upon the
subject whom he holds under his influence. He may
ask the question: "Do you see that mansion on the
hill,"—pointing in some given direction—"with its
beautiful surroundings? See! the foliage of the trees,
how chaste and delicate, and the many colored clusters of fragrant flowers, how sweet and pretty!"

"*Oh yes,*" *is the enthusiastic response,* "*I see them;*

*it's really the most facinating scene that I ever beheld.
I wonder whose mansion it is."*

Thus the psychology is definitely impressed with
the thoughts and conceptions of the person who exer-
cises a conscious mental influence over him, and his
coinciding views and rapturous expressions afford the
most positive evidence that the subjects vision is in
unison of perception with the *reflections* and *will* of his
magnetizer.

In and by this method it is shown to be possible to produce delightful visions of *unreal* scenes in
the mind of the subject of psychology, which is a
result growing out of the contact of the elements
of mentality under the exercise of will, as between
man and man in external life.   Now, if this be so,
may it not be equally true that the "immortals," our
friends and relatives in spirit life, who are presumed
to retain their identity and powers of mind unim-
paired after death, although unseen and perhaps at
some distance from our location, are able to so attune our thoughts, so control our intellectual and
semi-intellectual faculties, our emotions, passional inclinations, motives and desires, as to produce the
many dreams and realizations which are experienced
in the state of sleep and in semi-wakeful consciousness by the majority of mankind.

When I became old enough to reason concerning
my own condition, and to observe the peculiarities
manifested in the *Absenteeism* of my Father s mind,
he being a very intemperate thinker upon all subjects
of interest, and in a state of trance-like reflection
almost constantly, I could then much better realize

the marvelous characteristics of my own experience, and could readily understand that I was in possession of the fruits of inherited somnambulism, like Himself, my Brother and other members of our family; and that for some cause, *at the time to me unknown,* I was a very susceptible subject of remarkable impressions, visions and thoughts, which in almost every instance seemed to be imparted to my mind with wondrous order and precision, as if intended for an intimation, notification or some personal benefit, and as if directed by some *calculating and intelligent cause.*

When I was eleven years old, and during my school-boy days, I formed a habit—which was sometimes rather overdone—of leaving my Father's roof after tea time, and of running away to the village, which was some half mile distant from our residence. There I would engage in various sports and pastimes with the boys of my age and acquaintance, and would remain until late at night, playing "tag," "pom-pom-pull-away," or "hide and seek," when tiring of the games and frolisome diversions in which I delighted, I would leave my comrads and run like a "timid hero" that I was, toward home through the darkness.

Upon one occasion, it being a beautiful moonlight evening, and the boys seeming to feel more like play than usual, it was proposed and settled upon among them to engage in the artful and athletic sport of "hunting the grey fox." The author of the suggestion to enlist in this pleasurable recreation, was a young man of agreeable disposition, possessing great physical endurance and firmness of mind. It was for this

reason that he was chosen to fulfill the arduous labor de-
volving upon the wary and lubricious "grey fox" in the
chase of that delightful evening over the hills and
through the valleys, about our native village. We had
been running nearly an hour, sections of our little party
dividing off and separating in various directions, to
accomodate a more scrupulous search for the "leader,"
who had thus far successfully eluded the vigilance
of his pursuers, when, through a circumstance, in
following up a narrow ravine which was overhung
with forest trees, and which was not far from my
Father's residence, I lost every companion in the
merry chase with the exception of one. Together
we two—having concluded that further running and
search was useless—walked leisurely along through
the fields until we reached a private roadway which
led across some pasture lands and ran under the hills
beside a piece of woods, when making our course
toward home, and just as we were walking up
an embankment which led out to the main road,
and which was behind a large promontory in front
of our position, we were both surprised as well
as puzzled to observe an old vacated shanty, which
belonged to my Father and which had been locked
up for some time, presenting a bright illumination
at its western window.   In our surprise we
halted for a moment to look at the shining light
which was distinctly visible, when I remarked to my
companion with a feeling of anxiety:

"It's very singular that a light should appear in
the old shanty at this time o'night. I know my
Father keeps a lock on the door. I wonder if some-

body has'nt crawled in through the window to play cards or stay over night."

Turning about with a slight shrug of the shoulder, as if somewhat perplexed in mind, he replied:

"I hardly know what to think of it, Marcene," —using the abreviated name by which I was called —"it can't be the light of the moon, for that's rising in the east, and the window, which we see, is on the west side of the building, and beyond the reach of its rays."

Remaining silent for a moment, he again remarked, and this time with an evident air of timidity, which, I must confess, that as a boy I also to some degree experienced:

"I guess, it's a mysterious affair, and we'd better go away."

Starting together to pass around the brow of the hill which led to the highway, not more than sixty rods distant from my father's house, we now unexpectedly met one of our happy party, who, having heard our voices, came around to meet us on the road. As he approached us, we directed his attention to the shanty which was still brilliantly lighted up, when he very facetiously ejaculated:

"That's an *almighty* curious thing."

At this moment the thought came to my mind that, as there were three of us—our courage of course being naturally augmented by our numbers—it was our duty to go and see if we could discover the cause of the illumination, and so I said:

"Come now, say we go up toward the building and see for ourselves who or what there is in it."

One of the boys made no reply, but evinced an inclination not to gratify my wishes by turning to go in the opposite direction, while the other, not more brave perhaps, but greatly more given to off-hand witticism and ready retort, very suggestively remarked:

"Dev'l take the shanty, I guess it's bewitched." When with a very satisfied air he too turned to go away, and as my *scarry sensations* were very prominent at that particular moment, I made no *hesitation* about keeping pace with him in the retreat from that ghostly locality.

We had now reached a point on the road which brought my Father's residence plainly to view, and as it was getting to be quite late in the evening, I bid my companions "good night," and went directly home. It was half past eleven o'clock, and no one was up of all our family, with the exception of my mother, who was patiently waiting my return, while industriously engaged in knitting a pair of coarse woolen stockings for some member of the household. As I entered the room where she was sitting, still in a flame of excitement over what I had seen, I very quickly remarked:

"Oh, mother! Don't you believe that as three of us boys were coming round the hill to night, up on the farm road, we saw the Old Shanty all lit up."

"You'r a simpleton," said she with a distrustful smile, "your father locked the door and fastened the windows some time ago, and no one can get into it. I guess, you'd better go to morrow and look again, and see how easy it is to be mistaken."

I saw at once that my mother was incredulous, and inclined to discourage in me the trust in that knowledge which I supposed that I actually possessed, and so I said:

"I'm satisfied that the shanty was lighted up, for I saw it with my own eyes, and so did the other boys, and in the morning I'm going up there to see if the door is fastened."

"Well," she replied, "you can do that, but you won't find anything more than an empty hovel."

Perceiving that there was no hope of convincing her of the truth of what I had related, and feeling somewhat weary, as a result of the evenings rambles, I now took a candle from the long mantle which was near me, and with a singular sense of disappointment and mortification over what I had seen, and what had been said, I at once, as upon the occasion of my vision of the child, hastened to my sleeping apartment, and taking to my bed was soon lost in unconscious slumber.

Dear reader, what do you think became of the lonely Old Shanty behind the hill. It was on Thursday evening that we saw the bright light which appeared at its window. The day following I visited the house and found the door closed and safely locked against all intruders, and everything about it seemed to be in good order and undisturbed. The evidence of its having been illuminated or occupied by strangers on the previous night was very meager indeed, in view of external proof to the contrary, and owing to my inability at that time, and as an inexperienced youth, to reason consecutively concerning the phenomena which I had beheld, in any light in which it might be regarded, I began to think that perhaps I was altogether mistaken.

Friday and Saturday passed, and Sunday came with a pleasant smile to greet and cheer the weary toilers of the earth. On that day I wandered from home, over the hills and through the forest, far to the south of our family residence, being accompanied thither by a friendly acquaintance, whose general disposition and sportive tendencies of mind I had ever admired and held in the highest estimation. We traveled some four miles together to the place where my associate had made an appointment to meet a relative for the purpose of adjusting some little matter of business which had arose between them, and being detained until late in the afternoon, it was nearly dark when—after what became to me a very tiresome walk—we passed along the road which led by the Old Shanty on our homeward-bound journey. Owing to what had transpired in that locality on the previous Thursday night, I inadvertantly turned my head and looked in that direction, but observed no change in the appearance of the building or its surroundings.

Feeling weary on my return home, I reclined upon a lounge, which formed a part of the furniture of our sitting-room, and was resting in ease and comfort as the darkness came on. I had been enjoying this state of quietness and repose for something like an hour, when suddenly and simultaneously I heard several voices crying *fire! fire! fire!*

At this moment, also, my mother came into the

apartment where I was resting, and in a great flurry of excitement exclaimed:

"Marcenus, the Old Shanty is all in flames."

I at once arose to my feet, secured my coat and hat, and in a state of mental surprise and agitation, characteristic of a boy, ran up the road and climbing the hill, upon the side of which the building stood, watched the fiery flames for an hour or longer, with thirty or forty other persons who had gathered around the scene from different portions of the neighborhood, until nothing remained of the Old Shanty, save a quantity of ashes and a few dying embers.

The opinion obtains in our day, more than in former times, that "ministering spirits," possessing ample ability, and in a manner which we cannot readily comprehend, are enabled to make known their presence, and demonstrate their kindly sympathy in human interest, by watching us in our trials and struggles for happiness and the maintainance of being, and by warding off many of the misfortunes which inevitably make their appearance, and are met with as stumbling blocks and hinderances to success in the journey of life. That there is abundant evidence of the truth of such a belief no one well acquainted with the "history of phenomena" can reasonably question.*

The human mind naturally obtains and appropriates that kind of information which it most desires and seeks. It was ever my inclination to rest a

* The reader is referred to a work entitled the "Night side of Nature," by Catherine Crow; and another, "Modern American Spiritualism," by Emma Harding Brittan.

hope, if not to yield absolute confidence to a belief in the reality of many forewarnings and the verification of them in subsequent circumstances and events. Thus the instance of the incendiary burning of the Old Shanty, as well as other methodically represented incidents of a similar mysterious nature, which came under my personal observation in after years, or a knowledge of which was derived from historical date, only tended the more strongly to confirm my judgment in the truth and value of such a conviction.

The human mind is naturally involved in superstition, and hence inclined to a supercilious and willful rejection of such events and phenomenal evidences, as seem to partake of the marvelous or hold a place in the rank of so called "incrutable manifestations." The prejudices which we entertain, and which are built up under false schooling in the domestic circle and abroad in society, and which withall are coaxed and flattered by the Absaloms of creedal or theological interests, shut away all righteous freedom of thought from our desires, and subdue the intellect to a state of awe-stricken blindness and submission. To follow these prejudices, to cling to preconceived ideas and opinions, which have been fostered and fathered by the ignorant and designing through ages of time, is the fault of the world. The released understanding seeks no guards for the defense of long-cherished views. The privilege of a belief in what our forefathers taught, is not so acceptable as the same or similar knowledge received through the use of our own senses. The scepter which we hold in our own hands is better for our use than that which served a patriarch or prophet of primitive generations. If we wish to control a horse or make him our servant, we hamper his power of resistance, and subdue his will to the purposes of our ambition. *He never forgets the training.*

Oh! how mistaken are they who allow the children of their hearts to be subdued in intellect, or frustrated in that holy freedom of mind which appoints and substantiates its own knowledge, and guarantees everlasting individual satisfaction in life.

The mysterious incidents which announce themselves as an evidence of fore-warning, or which seem to indicate impending danger to property or mortal life, are quite as common as the occurrance of circumstances converging to such a necessity would seem to warrant. The lights seen in unoccupied houses; the shadowy forms which sometimes unexpectedly flit across our vision, and then as suddenly disappear; the unwelcome sound which surprises us just previous to the decease of some near and dear friend or relative; the moving of some article of furniture within our dwelling; the haunted chamber; the trailing of silk in the darkness, or the hollow guttural utterance issuing from some vacant room or darksome corner: all are but so many surprises, bespeaking the presence and nearness of unseen individual beings, who produce these various demonstrations, either for our special benefit in cases of sickness, sorrow and personal emergency, or as a reminder to prompt us to the performance of more worthy deeds in life, and to the exercise of executive reflection concerning matters which pertain to a super-mundane realm of realities, powers and personalities.

The detestable habit which many people adopt through fear, favor or prejudice, of secreting the truth to accomodate some established and petted theory in ethics, art, science or philosophy, or of hiding the ever-forthcoming revelations of nature to serve some selfish purpose in finance or the devotional relationships of society, is privately as well as publicly mischievous and hurtful, and is a most unmanly subterfuge to use in the pursuit of intellectual occupations and desires. Men are not consistent who commit themselves to silence to accomodate a neighbor's self-conceived wisdom, or the still more domineering presumption of some whittled-out advocate of theological precepts. Mind, edged by the friction of experience, or corrected through the force of its own mistakes, follies and dependence in being, is indeed *saved* in the temple of nature. Whereas *advised* goodness—like rain-drops upon the feathers of a bird— is happily received without injury, but its superficial influence is ever more engrossing to courtesy and the imagination than substantial in its tendency to promote the better interests of the soul.

CHAPTER III.

BOYHOOD DAYS. MENTAL INFLUENCES. NATURE.

It was my inclination in my boyish days to seek the solemn silence and retirement which were alone to be found in the dark and shadowy recesses of the woods, or in the more delightful places of repose beneath the green-clad trees of the open fields; and when I was obliged to attend school, which was generally adverse to my desire, it was my custom to remain in the company of my school-fellows only so long as they were quiet and free from those tantalizing and mischievous purposes which are so often the fault of the young, making them objectionable as companions, and frequently rendering manhood and womanhood in after time as unstable, as in all possibility it is likely to become insecure and infelicitous.

I only continued at school in all about five years, and while I was not altogether inapt in the pursuit of my studies, or neglectful of the many duties which were there imposed upon me, I still felt a great reluctance to comply with the toilsome and tedious methods of mental dicipline, which in those days—some thirty years ago—it was the custom to impose upon the young student. .

The old stone house where I attended school is
no longer in existence, the materials of which it was
composed having been conveyed away to make room
for a more commodious structure. But the memories
which still cling around that never-to-be-forgotten
place of education, where the joys and cares of my
early life were first made clearly manifest, are still
as fresh as ever; and when I contemplate those
long-departed days, and think of those with whom it
was my pleasure then to associate, I am only caused
to realize that gratefulness of heart which results
from a recollection of the past, and those my play-
mates, some of whom having attained maturer years,
long since passed onward to the blessed realm of the
spirit, or otherwise still remain to bless that "old
acquaintance" in the life which is of the earth.

During the years of childhood my mind gathered
up a treasure of singular interior realizations. Dreams
and visions of a peculiar character were imparted to
my memory. Strange sensations, impulses and emotions were *imposed* upon me from some unknown
source, and sometimes my *thoughts* seemed *caught* and
carried along, or were held to some needful interest
with unusual tenacity of purpose. Then again becoming released, I would feel comparatively easy and
contented in spirit, being left wholly free to perform
the monotonous drudgery of every day life without
psychologic emotion or molestation.

When we consider the great diversity of genius,
of power, of purpose, represented in the characteristics of the human mind, we may not regard it, after
all, as so very surprising that certain persons should

at times give expression to more than ordinary intelligence, should possess wondrous discernment or manifest acute spontaneity in the exercise of mental gifts
and privileges; for it is evident to every person
of discretion that the phrenological faculties, or the
various sections of thought and feeling in the brain,
may be so acted upon and influenced ante-natally,
educationally and psychologically, as to cause them
to diverge from the course of orderly development
or expression, and become the basis of some special
or marvelous mental manifestation, as in the case
of Cora Wilburn or young Safford, either of whom
could solve the most difficult problems in mathematical science with instantaneous and never-failing precision.*   Then again we have the case of Blind Tom,
the remarkable musician, whose inordinate stupidity in
other respects was ever quite as observable as his talent
for the spontaneous execution of musical discords and
consonance.   These are instances of mental illumination wherein certain faculties domineer to the abuse
of harmony in the *Renezuen* elements of thought.

The brain of man is a compound organic association of material particles, and from inherited or extraneous causes, is more likely to present a partial
than a uniform development of its energies and activities.   Hence, mind may rise to distinction as a
result of the unfoldment of some special faculty, or

---

* When the mind is thus peculiarly developed it is easily
impressed in its strongest sense by unseen intelligent powers,
and that without arousing any personal consciousness or realization of the influx of thought or intelligence with the individual
who is the subject of such influence.

receiving the impulse of evenness in its expansion, it may become attuned to the condition of the most perfect illumination in clairvoyance.

Mind cannot be released from its association with brain substance during the life of the body, but in moments of slumber, when will is inactive, and the elements of thought are calm and undisturbed; then with the *gentle touches* of another's *will* and *thoughts*, whether the operator be a *man* or a *spirit*, there may be aroused within the thus reposing faculties the most beautiful and heavenly, or the most horrible and distressing dreams and visions.

A spirit Brother, Sister, Father or Mother, floating in the currental streams of the atmosphere, far above our location upon the earth, may in their loving kindness look down upon us when we sink to rest at night, and approving of our lives, commend us to the delight of interior consciousness and a sight of scenes more joyous and grand than language is capable of describing, or wishing to correct our faults they may play a tune of distress upon our mental faculties as easily as the pianist would execute a note of discord upon his instrument.

In case of clairvoyant development the adjacent interblending hemispheres of thought are invariably in a uniform condition of unfoldment and activity, their combined elements being easily moved by psychologic processes as a result of their wondrous flexibility. The eyes in such case are easily closed at the option of a foreign will, and life, energy, reason and every sense of the soul is held in abeyance of a foreign control to conditions of vivaciousness or inactivity. While reposing in this *interior* state of peace and quietness, the mind receives new ideas and impressions, and the senses becoming singularly acute, are abnormally aroused to the experience of strange realizations. Visions as beautiful and perfect as stereoscopic pictures are imparted to and impressed upon its inner consciousness, while its reception of intelligence from *unseen* sources becomes a matter of every day experience.

Spiritual philosophy demonstrates what all history asserts and logical inference guarantees, that mind is acted *upon*, and is psychologically subject *to* the will-force of invisible, intelligent beings, who influence, move or animate its organic functions, alike to the surprise of the understanding, as to the advantage or disadvantage of human welfare.

One of the most singular instances of spirit influence and control on record is presented in the *Renezun* epidemic, called the "Dancing mania of the middle ages," and which appeared at intervals during the thirteenth and fourteenth centuries. At Aix-la-Chappelle, the capital of a district in Rhinish-Prussia, during the summer months of the year thirteen hundred and seventy-four, there appeared assemblies of men and women upon the streets screaming and foaming like persons "possessed." The dancers losing all control over their individual movements, went into paroxisms of maniacal delight, and often into delirium of mind in their involuntary activity. They danced and they leaped, they yelled and hooted, wept and sung; until falling in extreme exhaustion they would groan and moan, as if in the agonies of death. Some tore their hair and mutilated their persons, while others dashed out their brains against solid walls in their psychologic madness. Men rushed from place to place with phrensy and evil visions haunted their minds. Troops of dancers wandered hither and thither followed by crowds of people, who taking the supposed infection poured out their imprecations against the priests, even going so far as to take possession of their houses of worship, and driving them through the streets in terror.*

The excitement called the "Dancing Mania" was regarded as a contagious influence, but reason as based upon a knowledge of the psychologic laws which control mind accepts no such conclusion, in view of the fact that mind alone was effected, and no disease accompanied its manifestations.

The world will be made wiser when the laws governing the senses are better understood. When it is known that the "realms of the invisible" are peopled by a *Liv-le-un* host, who are able to wield a wondrous mental power over not only individuals, but whole communities of men, for a purpose wise or otherwise, it may be our joy, as well as our benefit, to accept a privilege in better consideration concerning those mysterious physical and mental manifestations which have occurred in all ages, and which have proved to be as much a source of distress as of hope to the human heart in its search for a knowledge of immortal life.

The Convulsionaries of France who appeared during the seventeenth century, afford another instance

*Spirits in mockery of the world's theology.

of the effect of those psychologic powers which the systematic logic of the harmonial philosophy alone enables us to explain, as having a substantial origin in the action of *Spirit will-force,* as exercised in control of the elements of the human mind. It is related that this singular sect threw themselves into the most violent convulsions, rolled about upon the ground, imitated birds, beasts and fishes, and at last, when they had completely exhausted their vital powers, went off in a swoon, becoming entranced and insensible.

When men seek wisdom and find that felicity which is to be secured in freedom of thought and reasonable consideration; when domineering theology and its abettors no longer impose upon the good sense of mankind or the "immortals," who live in the enjoyment of the peaceful pleasures which are to be secured in that Mansion "not made with hands, which hangs suspended in the heavens:" then in justice to an awakened sense of human equality, of right and wrong, as practically exemplified in personal conduct and the governments of men, the loving children of the sky will release humanity from psychologic torments.

Salem witchcraft was a punishment awarded to the "blue lights" of "high theology" from the Spirit sphere. Men went mad in derision of their own folly and self-conceit, and the "Hint" which they received from the *Woteun** reserve on the downy *Marno†*

---

* The place of legislation in the superior realm which is associated with American interests.

† An aereal stratum where spirits live in much happiness.

C

of the air, while it served as a check to religious in-
tolerance, was lost in historic renown, and the *Tal-
avans* of Sectarianism are still alive with their fiery
Gehenna as needful to the correction of a wicked
people's morals.

Every age has had its mysterious movements.
The swoomings and the jerkings, the dancings and
the jumpings, are so many evidences of men's folly.
When we are culpably ignorant of every law of life,
following the superstitious imagery and teachings of
artful and designing craftsmen, and ignoring the ad-
vantages secured by freedom in educational training,
we may expect to be wrought upon by every bug-
bear of hallucination, and "the spirits of just men
made perfect," may look down with indifference upon
the *Dewonvies** of the sub-stratums of the atmosphere,
and smile in their wisdom, while

The effects of psychology as practiced by them,
Makes Jerry Madidlers and jerkers of men.

It is high time that we had learned the wondrous lesson which has been given for our benefit in
the manifestations of mind as developed through the
influence of this most marvelous principle, or as made
practicle for good or ill results in human life, through
the designs of unseen, intelligent beings, our own
kith and kind, perhaps, of the spirit world. For centuries mankind have contended over theological privileges, rites and ceremonies, and contemning every
precept of wisdom as derived from the study of mental

---

* Those who have permanent guardian cares, and who influence—not necessarily always in wisdom—earthly friends by
mental methods.

science, they have wandered in the delightful labyrinths
of the imagination, and following the *Ignis fatui* of
fancy, they have become mystified and confused in
understanding, or lost to individual advancement and
progress as a result of their adherence to the delu-
sions of sectarian cliques and clans.

Nature, the source and support of life, the basis
of all law, the only thing which *is*, and which fills
all time and space, is neglected in our contemplations,
and forgotten in our acceptance of insecure speculations and theories. The edicts of the Divine Spirit,
as registered in the "book of creation," and the many
lessons of wisdom so generously offered in its pages
are lost sight of, and the happiness which we otherwise might enjoy is infringed upon by the absolutism
and bigotry thus engendered.

Nature gave life to man; gave all that man enjoys; gave law, consciousness, power, privilege, circumstance and immortality. The eye sees nature by
natural means. The ear hears as a result of the
vibratory action of atmospheric elements upon the
tympanum and its nerve connections. Mind may
with propriety be regarded as a contemplative mirror
wherein is reflected the diversified objects and images
abounding in creation. Nature is ever free in her
gift of evidence, impartial in her bestowment of' use-
ful lessons of instruction, and cancels no righteous
claim to liberty. Theology, on the contrary, hampers
our opinions, confines our thoughts and actions to
the limit of a "select purpose," and to "formal ceremonies, holds the mind to a "selfish hope" through a
love for "exclusive association," and banishes a gen-

crous purpose in the exercise of a noble sympathy for humanity, by cramping and restricting our views and sentiments.

Nature is the pride of every roving school child, and guarantees satisfaction to all. In the examination of her flowers, trees, fruits, and diversified forms, they find happiness and learn wisdom. Not so with the sectarian teachings of men. Nay, mind is belittled by exclusiveness and bigotry, and the clearer perceptions of the intellect are greatly befogged through a manifestation of selfishness in the selection and adoption of religious opinions. Nature is a freedom in the most singular extremes. She bestows upon the negro a colored skin, crisped hair, a flat nose, and a flatter foot. Upon the white man she confers a more slender form, with features of happier mould, and a skin of ample whiteness. To the Patagonian giant she imparts a wondrous physical power. To the Aztec, a body of weak and delicate proportions.

Nature is a joy to every human soul. Is a success to those who read her lessons aright and comprehend their meaning. She has given to man the highest worldly position and power; to the angels of the spirit *Paradi*, the most unmeasured wisdom. Her ways are mostly reliable and secure. Under her guidance the populations of the earth find their varied geographical locations, while through her decision the heights of the surrounding atmosphere, above each terrestrial nation, becomes the dwelling place of the *Livle* of our planets production—men and women born to immortality, and who once lived and enjoyed that condition which *we*, their terrestrial successors, have also received as our inheritance, and which in time must, as well with us, eventuate in our release from all mortal relationships, trials and difficulties. Standing amid the flowing elements which trace their course around the outskirts of the aereal ocean far beyond the clouds, the time-appointed children of men send their thoughts to the four winds of heaven, and to the four corners of the globe which revolves beneath their feet, and all through an understanding of the principles of mind, and the means of controlling it which is accorded to their intelligence. Men are made to psychologically dance and sing, weep and mourn, shake like the Quakers, ramble in prayers and swoon in religious supplication, all at the instigation of a wisdom or design wholly hidden and inscrutable.

Many christian people imagine that spirits are at once made perfect when released from mortal confinement. That death cures our folly, makes us happy, peaceful, quiet, loving, kind, generous and just. This is not nature's excellence, it is not her decision; for she rides the tempest in abusive commotion, and garners her peace amid the changes of creation. She overshadows the earth with darkness, yet concedes a joyous privilege in varied realizations to all life, during the delightful hours of the open day.

Nature is an equilibrium bounded by two extremes. She organizes innumerable forms from her store of chemical elements, and secures their dissolution through the *Garnee* of death and decay. Our truest happiness is alone secured through obedience to truth, while misery is prompted and mingles its

mischief and abuse in self-corrective doses to suit the
patrons of folly, and those who refuse a joy in life's
"better way."

The culprit carries the characteristics of his
earthly condition with him to the *Perfiresta* of the
future life, where he lives to subdue the personal
faults and imperfections which pertain to his being.
Mind is not responsible for its defects, no more than
is the physical body for its oft mis-shapen mould.
We cannot avoid the inheritance of vice, neither the
love of aspiration. The intellect is never perfect, but
is always in desire to improve. Our intelligence increases, but by slow degrees. We gather wisdom as
the little bee gathers the honey from the flowers. It
has to go into many dark places, escape many narrow chances of life, and select its food from many
objectionable plants; still, it never tires, is ever earnest, dilligent and dutiful, wandering hither and
thither to accomplish the purposes of its existence,
or to serve the demands of its being.

So with the human mind: slowly but surely it
accomplishes its purpose, or attains the object held in
its desire. By continuous thought upon any subject
the intellect becomes enlarged and expanded. When
a person yearns to understand those things which
pertain to the exalted life of the future, and the desire thus entertained is prompted by a worthy motive, it is almost certain that its proper and legitimate
gratification will ultimately follow.

CHAPTER IV.

A VIVID DREAM. HOME CONVERSATIONS.
GINGER - BREAD VISIONS. A FATHER'S
COUNSEL.

The knowledge which I possessed of the nature
or philosophy of the human mind at the period to
which I have hereinbefore referred, was very limited,
and the "duplex visions," "aereal flights" and singular
dreams which I then frequently received were to my
understanding equally a source of wonder and surprise, and as a result of the indifference of others in
regard to a relation of the details of such experience, and
the many pooh-poohs which were uttered upon the suggestion of the probability of spirit influence in their
production, I seldom considered it discreet or advic-
able to speak of them. Hence they were safely
treasured in the quiet recesses of my memory to be
more particularly regarded in after years, or partially
forgotten, as a result of personal unconcernedness or
close attention to business occupations.

When I was in my twenty-fourth year of age,
and upon an occasion when not in the least anti-
cipated, it being in the early twilight of the morning,

I became suddenly and deeply entranced, as a result
of the action of some foreign influence upon my mental faculties while yet I was reposing in quiet and
unconscious slumber. I had been dreaming, and my
vision was carried to many scenes of beauty and
interest I wandered beside the gently flowing waters
of a forest enfolded stream, where the genial warmth
of a tropical sun had induced nature to clothe many of
her diversified forms with perpetual green. Along its
banks grew the most attractive variety of fragrant
flowers. The bending trees hung in quietness above
the placid surface of the brook, casting their broad
limbs and leaf-covered branches in deep and accurate
reflection below.

As I was contemplating my situation, or gazing
in admiration upon the splendor of the scene which
surrounded me, I all at once heard a low, moaning
sound in the distance, which seemed to proceed from
some one who was in the fullest grief of heart, and
who was endeavoring to give expression to the deep
sense of sorrow which was experienced. Turning
about in the direction of the sound which I had
heard, and observing a narrow pathway leading
through the thicket, I at once sought refuge behind
a large oak tree, which secreted me from observation while I listened to the sad, discomforting
words, which were uttered by some one who seemed
to be gradually approaching my location.

I had not long remained in watchful and secret
observation in the quiet and secluded place which I had
chosen for my retreat, when looking in the direction
from whence the pathway issued, I saw two persons

walking slowly toward me. I gazed attentively at
them as they neared my position, and was equally
surprised and astonished to behold a colored man
and woman seeking the sources of peace and freedom
as fugitives in the unseen retirement of the woods.
Not far from the embowered spot where I was confined, and just beside the trodden path which they
were following, lay a large fallen tree. Approaching
this, and seating themselves upon its body, the woman, while yet in seeming anguish of heart, broke
forth in a lay of melodies sadly chosen in explanation of her trials, sufferings and prospective separation from a companion selected in the love and sympathy of her soul. The tawny negro by her side
was the hope of her life, but the misfortune of being
parted from him was now apparently eminent. A
slave mart was her distress. The bloodhounds were
on his track. As he sat by her side in that lonely
place in the forest with depressed and drooping spirits, yet with a will to avoid his relentless pursuers,
he looked backward in the direction from which he
had come, and with a look of defiance very sternly
remarked :

"I will evade them along the *shaae.*"

When taking her by the hand and pressing it in
his own, as he arose to make his escape, directing
his course toward the brook which he had named,
he broke forth in low and solemn, yet happy accents
of vocalization, selecting the beautiful air of "The
Watcher" to give expression to his sense of suffering
and his affection for the wife of his choice in song.
As I stood surprised and almost transfixed, in the

stillness and silence of the peaceful ambuscade which
I had selected as a place of safety and observation,
I could hear the final notes of music as they floated
on the air, and were lost in suppressed echos among
the hills and valleys along the uneven pathway
which he was pursuing. The last sound of his voice
conveyed to my ear these words:

> "We'll part no more, dear Mena,
> Upon this earthly shore."

Feeling interested in the music thus heard, I
continued to listen for some time, thinking that perhaps I might hear something further or see something more to awaken my attention or arouse my
curiosity, when all at once I seemed to be released
from the entranced condition in which I had beheld
the vision, and looking about, as my normal consciousness became partially restored, I observed that
I had risen while in sleep, and in *semi-deshabille* was
penning the words of the song which I had heard.

I sat upon the edge of the bed which I occupied
and was earnestly engaged with my pencil writing,
upon a stand which stood at its head, the two con-
cluding lines of the sentimental ballad which was
sung by the flying fugitive, when I awoke. As my
outward memory became fully aroused, and I began
to realize my situation, my wife who had been disturbed in her slumbers by my movements and uneasiness, suddenly ejaculated:

"What in the world are you about? It's not
time to rise. Why, you've been acting like a witch
for an hour."

Feeling somewhat mortified over my own condition of mind, yet experiencing a sense of pleasure, as a result of my somnambulic realizations, I very indifferently replied:

"*I hardly know myself what I am about.* I only know that I was dreaming and listening to vocal music, and as I awoke, I discovered myself seated here by the stand writing the lines of poetry which I heard sung."

"That's very singular," she remarked, "perhaps you'd better lay down and rest again, as you've been so much disturbed."

"Oh, no," said I, "the twilight of the morning begins to light up the eastern sky, and as I feel that I could get no sleep after so impressive a dream as that which I have just awoke from, I guess I'll clothe myself and prepare for the duties of the day."

Making my actions accord with my words, I at once dressed myself, and leaving the room, went down stairs, took some pails from the pantry, and went out to milk in a little yard near by. My mind was not at rest. I kept busy attending to the various chores which were assigned to my care, and which are ever a part of the labor of farm-life; still I could not refrain from reflection concerning the mysterious amplifications of thought, and the strange, yet definite scenes which were forever arising in my mind during the quiet hours of sleep. Many times I would find myself in conversation with entire strangers, living in the woods, among the hills and valleys, then again in the palaces of the rich, with a heart as full and free as if no care ever overshadowed the human heart. Sometimes sorrow would clothe my night-wanderings with her mantle of distress, and I would awake from my slumbers in a flood of tears.

"What," said I, "has mind the capacity to rob itself of joy? Wherefore are the mental faculties moved to activity in a consciousness wholly abnormal, yet which in many particulars has every sense characteristic of outward realizations."

"Can mind run away with itself," I mentally inquired, "and get into all sorts of jumbles, difficulties, joys, happinesses and fructification of its own ideas. Some people think that dreams are of no account. I wonder who ever heard of a railroad train running from place to place without the directing care of an engineer. Is mind self-poised? Is it organically formed? Yes, thought I, it cannot be otherwise, if it is a counterpart of the natural brain and the nerves of sensation."

Thus I continued to reason with myself as I labored betimes milking the cows, feeding the horses and pigs, and aiding my mother in the performance of some little duties about the house.

As the members of our family were seated at breakfast that morning, I took occasion to refer to the remarkable dream which I had experienced, and as I did so, I very frankly remarked:

"I wonder why it is that I am forever overdone in dreaming. Hardly a night passes that I do not realize pain or pleasure as a result of the abnormal activity of my mental faculties. What do you think, mother, is the cause of my thoughts being so restless when I sleep. I confess *my* inability to fathom the mystery."

Looking over her spectacles with a somewhat suggestive smile she unhesitatingly replied:

"That ginger-bread you eat so much of yesterday must have been the cause."

I could not refrain from a hearty laugh at this easy method of solving a highly metaphysical problem. It was my satisfaction however to see that while the facetious explanation thus given was altogether insufficient to account for my mental experience, that my own more serious reflections were quite as inadequate to establish the cause of the mental phenomena in question; hence I very deliberately answered:

"I am not satisfied with this oft-repeated interpretation of a subject which is really worthy of more serious thought. It is easy to say: "We will occupy a house," but it is not so easy to build a house to occupy, as this requires labor, capital and mechanical skill. Thus it is with the demonstration of all ideas, opinions and truth. We shy the logic of necessity to accommodate the idealisms of the imagination. We are but vague, indolent and listless reasoners, seeking conclusions in *assumption* rather than toil for credible knowledge in manly effort."

"The human mind," continued I, "in my judgment, is a mechanism of ethereal elements so nicely attuned to harmony in organic association, that like the notes of a musical instrument they may be moved to the expression of every emotion, and the actualization of every sense during the hours of slumber.

It is evident that mind cannot and would not instigate a punishment against itself, neither impoverish pleasures, interest itself in observation or assume moods of reflection, when normal consciousness is obtuse to the power of personal recognition, as when the soul rests in sleep. We must therefore conclude that the action of the "cogitative elements of mind" during such periods, is surely the result of an operative mesmeric force proceeding from some unseen intelligence, alike endowed with reason, calculation, and the several faculties which amplify ideas, and qualify the understanding in a knowledge of the method of inducing by psychologic processes—sensative thought, memory, hearing, seeing, tasting or eating—which is common in dreams—and smelling, together with the irregular and forced action of all the characteristic functions of the soul or spirit.

"It would be unwise" said I, in conclusion, "to adopt the opinion that dreams are merely the result of the self-appointed movements of mind unaided by *will* or *consciousness*—two of its most important principles. Yet it is very easy to perceive that when these two functions are at rest, the balance of the mind's powers may be subjected to the influence of a foreign will and gently controlled to the production of dreams, visions, and all the multiplied phenomena peculiar to the state of sleep, somnambulism and trance."

My Father, who was seated by my side, and who was ever interested in considerations which pertained to subjects of a metaphysical nature, having now finished his morning meal, leaned back in his chair and very advisingly remarked :

"Marcenus, it is well enough to reflect upon these subjects now and then, but I fear you are given to a too earnest thought in seeking to unravel the mysteries of mind in its various moods and states. I have reflected for years concerning my own experience as a somnambulist in my younger days, but I cannot say that I have arrived at anything like a definite understanding in regard to the cause or causes which converged to its production, and I am quite well satisfied that while it may be possible to explain the *evidences* of mental phenomena, the basic law of soul-life is so deeply laid in mystery that the difficulty of securing a knowledge of its origin and more hidden manifestations must ever necessitate its remaining a "hobby" for the disputation of religionists, thinkers and metaphysicians."

"When I was a young man," he continued, "it was a circumstance of almost nightly occurrence with me to rise in my sleep and wander about in my Father's house. I would unconsciously leave my bed and without clothing upon my person seek the comfort of a large open fire-place in the old log dwelling in which we lived. Upon hearing the noise of my oft misdirected footsteps, or observing me through the darkness, some member of our family would wake me from my entranced condition of mind, and I would again return to my bed. During the hours of my sleep-walking I was usually impressed with the idea of driving horses and cattle, or of being out in the woods without any substantial object, of aid-

ing my Father in farming, and of having many fanciful duties to perform which were at times seemingly
entertaining and agreeable. To you it may seem
desirable to traverse the realms of fancy in pursuit
of the wondrous phenomena of mind, but as you
advance in years I think you will see—what I think
I realize—that the object of your search and anxiety
is altogether unattainable."

My Mother, who was ever ready to invent a
motive for the opinions expressed in home discourse,
now looked up very significantly and directing her
remarks to me, said:

"How long, Marcenus, are you and Father going
to converse about spooks and dreams. You'll never
agree on the subject if you continue talking till
dooms-day."

"Well, Mother," I answered, "I am ready to
quit at any time. It is true I differ with Father in
my conclusions in regard to the cause of dreaming,
and the ability of the mental faculties to reach an
understanding thereof; but I guess our difference of
views will never lead to any serious rupture of good
feeling; indeed I rather prefer to listen to his objections to my theories and speculations than otherwise."

Thus, in good nature, our conversation ended as
we finished our mornings repast, and I arose from
my seat and went out into the field to labor that
day with much joy, and many new and acceptable
ideas concerning the philosophy of dreams as a subject
wholly given to the mind in mystery.

CHAPTER V.

REFLECTIONS. THE ANCIENT PROPHETS. SWEDENBORG AND ANDREW JACKSON DAVIS.

Nearly every heart that beats in a mortal bosom longs for the continuation of life after death. The soul seeks happiness in a reverence for the unseen and the eternal. In the absence of reliable knowledge concerning the future destiny of the Spirit, men and nations have assumed fictitious garments of belief, and have selfishly ignored the commendable lessons which inevitably flow from "wise consideration" and liberality of thought.

When I was a boy, I wondered why it was that people differed so widely in their opinions upon religious subjects. In considering the state of society and the influence of ecclesiastical bodies over communities, I was invariably more puzzled and perplexed, than animated by a feeling of satisfaction, in view of their

variable teachings and anomalous characteristics. It
was the custom then as now for most persons to attend church upon the Sabbath day, and as my Father
was a clergyman, his family was necessarily under
obligation to follow his good counsel in that respect;
but still to my mind it was a singular manifestation
of human short-sightedness, if nothing worse, for
those who sought to worship the Divine Mind, or
grasp a comprehensive conception of angelic life, to
go selfishly here and selfishly there, in little cliques
and diminutive societies to establish and enjoy their
conflicting convictions.

Men are lacking in a knowledge of the truth,
thought I, as I grew older, for when I see them
worshiping Deity in an hundred ways, and contending over the propriety of their forms and ceremonies,
their various tenets of faith, and the ideas and sentiments which they entertain and cherish, I am satisfied that their differences are not authorized by the
wisdom of the Infinite Mind, but are rather the result
of a too exuberant hope, a slavish obstinacy in the
satisfaction of misconceived opinions, or of unreason-
ing confidence in the teachings of mistaken, yet
studied ministers of religion.

I could see no value in a system of thought or
morality which accommodated the rich, while the
poor and less intelligent were almost wholly neglected
or confined during worship to the uncushioned pews
in the rear of the synagogue. I heard the Baptists
deriding the views of the Methodists; the Presbyter-
ians quarreling with the Universalists and Unitarians,
while the whole Protestant world were malining the

character and deriding the religious precepts of the
Catholic Hierarchy. New religions and new forms
of worship were constantly appearing to put the final
finish upon supposed ultimate truth. The nimble
shakers danced and shook while the shameless mor-
mons foresook the most vital law of nature and
social life. Looking beyond my native land, I observed the savage and the heathen, thrice more
numerous than the christian, adopting other and
variable methods of satisfying their veneration for the
Omnipotent Being and the spirits of the departed.

As I contemplated the lesson thus awarded to
my preceptions; as I looked upon the conflict of human sentiment which sought refuge in a thousand
methods of expression, and which no mortal could
harmonize or correct, my heart was oppressed with
sadness, and I prayed for a truthful understanding
of nature's intention in the production and gift
of life.

Plodding on in the pathway of distrustful hope,
despairing of any success in the attainment of my
desires, I sought consolation in the study of the
characteristics of the human mind. I knew that I
was born a somnambule, that my Father and only
Brother were night-walkers, often rising from their
slumbers to accomplish the fanciful purposes conceived
of in dreams.

In looking over the pages of history I discovered
that a number of persons in past ages had claimed
to hold intercourse with beings of another world,
and had actually given some remarkable demonstrations of its truth, that is, providing the records con-

taining the statements and particulars in regard to
them and the evidence which they presented were in
any measure to be relied upon.

The scriptures, I remarked, were replete with
strong passages bearing directly upon this hidden and
difficult subject. Daniel, the magian, sage and philosopher, gave abundant proof of his ability to commune with the angel world, when through "fasting
and prayer" he became mentally entranced, or passed
into the "deep sleep" of clairvoyance, which seems
to have been very frequent during the entire period
of his earthly life.

Jacob and Ezekiel both enjoyed visions and spoke
with immortal beings, while Christ and St. John the
Revelator, endowed with more exalted knowledge,
amplified *interior* thought and observation, taught the
existence of spirits and angels, and referred to heaven
as the future home of the righteous upon earth.

Investigating still further the many claims made
to a freedom and familiarity in communion with the
beings of super-terrestrial spheres, I found that
Emanuel Swedenborg, the seer of Stockholm, had
presented more details concerning the future life, and
had held the lamp of mental illumination higher in
treating of the subject of the abode of spirits, their
characteristics and condition, than all the soothsayers,
prophets, sages and thinkers of antecedent generations.

I was more pleased, however, with the attested
facts proclaimed in the writings of Swedenborg
bearing upon his individual experience, than in the
multiform theories and speculations which, in the
deepest ambiguity of thought, he sought to establish.

While I could neither perceive the value nor understand the application of his interminable exegesis of
scriptural texts to the wants of the religious world,
I was quite well satisfied through a comparison of
certain stated facts concerning his intercourse with
spirits and the visions which he enjoyed, with the
similar realizations of others, that the demonstration
of the existence of invisible beings, and their near
relation to us, was perfect and indisputable.

In view of the many claims thus recognized and
acknowledged to a privilege so rare and wondrous as
that of speaking with the dead, and the ample testimony which history furnished in their confirmation,
I began to feel somewhat more easy in my mind in
regard to the safety of the spirit after its separation
from the physical form.

The death of my only Brother, which took place
when I was in my thirteenth year of age, had greatly
stimulated my desire to fathom, if possible, the state
of existence which in unseen silence he had inherited.
I felt that he was ever near, yet I could not readily
account for many of the impulses, emotions and feelings, which from time to time completely overshadowed my being. I had, however, adopted the
opinion that the *elements of thought*—mind substanti-
ating itself through organic centralization—were
either fundamentally insecure in their appointed *motions*, seeking actively in the absence of personal
consciousness, as when sleep holds the faculties in
forgetfulness of life, *pushing their sense of power* into
mutiny of manifest action, so to speak, or otherwise
in the calmness and tranquility which characterized

their condition during slumber, or in moments of peaceful reflection in wakeful hours they were gently influenced by psychologic will-force as supported in the discretion of "ministering spirits."

I was more fully confirmed in this opinion from reading a series of articles which appeared in some of the New York papers at the time of the introduction of Andrew Jackson Davis, the seer of Poughkeepsie, to public notariety as a subject of mesmerism and mental illumination. Mr. Davis was looked upon as the wonder of the world. His delivery of the articles contained in Nature's Divine Revelations attracted universal attention and called out the soldierly comments of the religious and secular press of the country.   ,

Although I was quite young at the time, I distinctly remember that my impressions were emphatically—as in the case of Swedenborg—more given to an interest in the experience of Mr. Davis as a subject of clairvoyance than to the philosophical exposition of "nature and her laws" which he presented in words more superabundant than prudent.

The phenomena of mind represented in his case greatly interested my thoughts. As I reflected concerning the peculiar power of wisdom which he manifested in his extemporaneous delivery of words and sentences without limit—he being at the time a boy only seventeen years old—I concluded that the human intellect was, indeed a *mystery*; but in view of his daily transition from external consciousness to psychologic slumber, and the masterly increase of knowledge which he evinced while in that condition, I conceived a satisfaction in thinking that the *mystery of mind* was not so great after all as to enable it to reach the fathomless depths of time and space, and to comprehend the mission of a universe, without a basis in the intelligence of *superior mind.* Andrew Jackson Davis was looked upon as a prodigy, his revelations as something marvelous. But how did he obtain the intelligence which he displayed? He could not make a disclosure of exalted knowledge without a source from which to obtain it. It was imparted to or became immerced in his thoughts and he gave oral expression to it while entranced and wholly unconscious.

Some said it was derived from other minds through contact and the law of sympathy. Others assumed that it was appropriated from the books of wise authors by some process of transmission not yet understood, while the seer himself affirmed that it was derived from a "great sphere of light" which contained "all conceivable knowledge," and which could be reached only in the most elevated state of clairvoyant illumination.

Amid the conflicting statements, theories and opinions, which were advanced by philosophers, logicians and writers, I came well nigh having no sentiment or idea of my own in regard to the matter, but of two things I was quite certain; first, that of those who assumed to know the most, and to be the readiest to render their explanations, there was generally the least substantial information to be gained. While as to the existence of the phenomena and the disclosures which were being made, I could only

arrive at one conclusion, that of the agency of disembodied mind in their production and presentation.

Mr. Davis had given to the world a volume
of thought which was not his own. He was a boy
in intellect, inexperienced and unschooled. His mind
could not *make* knowledge, but it could *receive* and
give expression to it. From whence did it originate?
Who was the responsible authority in its production?
Was it a quality of knowledge to float about in unseen and promiscuous quantities to be absorbed by
the sleeping intellect of an untaught youth? Letters
are usually obtained through dint of study and mental
effort, and the profound logician is expected to be a man
of learning. Not so with Mr. Davis, for he could
scarcely read or write; yet in his wondrous ability
as the subject of somnambulic sleep he was both
wordy and wise.

Wherefore, thought I, should Mr. Davis be
extolled as the "great author," the "wondrous seer,"
and "profound philosopher," when in his ordinary
condition he presents no evidence of superior perception, mental attainment or sagacity. There is a *secret*
involved in this permission of mind to receive intelligence from invisible sources. There are aids in Nature
which are ours when circumstances, well appointed,
prompt their actualization in human interest. This
influx of ideas into the understanding is the work
of unseen immortal beings, and in their love for
humankind they have chosen another Lazarus upon
whom to confer their woes.

The mystery which attaches to all, so called,
"supernatural manifestations," is evidently but a veil

of artful maneuverings employed—perhaps wisely—by the "invisibles" to daunt our efforts, or hide from our grasp that understanding which we all yearn to possess concerning "spiritual things."

The law of *mystery* is inseparably connected with all developments of a trans-mundane character, as well as all phenomenal representations of mental power. The appearance of apparitions, of ghosts and hobgoblins is ever appointed at an unexpected moment, and their withdrawal from human observation is equally as unlooked for and surprising. In all this there is more evidence of the presence, devise and consideration of invisible intelligences, than of willingness on their part to concede a familiarity to man, in an acquaintance with them, and their hidden condition of existence.

From reading and reflection I had now decided in my own mind the question of the truth of the immortality of the human soul. The testimony in favor of such a conclusion was overwhelming and incontrovertible. But where the disembodied spirit lived, how or why, were interrogatories as yet not fully settled to the entire satisfaction of my naturally doubting mind. The seers and prophets of all ages had, it. is true, intimated something in regard to the realities of another world, of a "heavenly sphere," of a "grand utopia" where life was supposed to be forever rendered secure and perfect. But still the amount of direct evidence was insufficient to establish anything like a clear and definite revelation, concerning the nature of the soul or the location of its place of abode in the future.

For weeks, months and years I deliberated upon
D

this and kindred subjects, feeling no impulse at any time to relinquish the more gratifying views of my own adoption; still, in realizing the fact that it was nearly, if not altogether impossible to solve the problem of the "destiny of the spirit" or to discover its place of abode, I was not wholly given to despair, although my heart went out in sadness, and I yearned through hope alone, for a better understanding of the objects and design of the Great Divine Author in the production and development of life.

CHAPTER VI.

THE PHENOMENA OF SPIRITUALISM. THE FOX FAMILY. A MOTHER'S ADVICE.

The "spirit rappings" which had now made something of a reputation as a "wondrous pheno- mena" or "marvelous mystery," began to be consi- dered by the press and in private circles in society, and were the theme of doubt, distrust, malignity and abuse on the one hand, while on the other a more generous, consistent and manly sentiment prevailed.

The Fox Family resided in the City of Rochester, New York, at the time to which I allude, and hundreds and thousands of people from all parts of the country were constantly arriving at their residence, there to hold communion with departed loved ones in the confidence of the heart, desiring to investigate the phenomena of spiritualism through motives founded in the deepest skepticism in regard to the future existence of the soul, or out of a pure intellectual ambition to solve a proposition in pneumatology, which was confounding the wisest *savants* and hetcheling theology out of its self-complacent languor.

The spirits were reported as being able to communicate words and sentences by means of the alphabet, and short messages were said to be thus frequently transmitted to inquiring earthly friends and relatives of the departed. They were able to rap in public halls, in strange houses, upon street pavements and in other places, and when subjected to the questionings of a committee of ladies which was chosen for that purpose, there was no lack. of sounds, notwithstanding the insulation of the *media* by means of glass tumblers, and their denudation in a room without fixtures or furniture which could in any way supply means for the practice of deception.

The singularity of the manifestations and the strange character which they presented had now become the subject of general remark, if not of unhappy comment, among not only the people who resided in the immediate vicinity of Rochester, but likewise with those living in all parts of the country,

who were curious for various reasons to listen to the
rappings, or gain access to a knowledge of the new
and so called "unaccountable developments" which,
if true, it was conceded, were the greatest blessing
ever offered to appease the incredulity of the mind
of man, or secure the happiness of the human heart,
while, if not true, they were certainly to be regarded
as the most wretched mockery of lies, tricks and
deceitful pettifogging ever conceived of in the interest of a most profound and serious subject.

Of course, without investigation I could form no
fixed or final opinion of my own in regard to the
matter, although I was not inclined to differ much
with those who averred in confidence, or who declared
in personal honor and sincerity their belief in the
spiritual origin of the sounds, and who assumed that
communion with another world was by this method
not only already realized, but likely in time to be
irrevocably established. Indeed, I held no settled
convictions upon the subject of the "mysterious
noises," but rather hoped that they were the result
of "wise design" on the part of the "immortals," our
own departed kindred, loving friends and relatives,
who were happier to grant us a knowledge—even
though meager in extent—of the condition of existence which it was theirs to inherit and enjoy.

Popular prejudice held no control over my mind,
and I felt no inclination to deride a system of phenomenal representations which I could so deeply
cherish, if true, neither had I any desire to misre-
present—as many seemed to have—the goodness,
generosity, native talent, disposition or characteristics

of the members of the family who seemed to be the specially chosen vehicle of their production. Although many of my neighbors and friends habitually laughed and sneered whenever the "mysterious noises" were referred to in conversation, or when the Fox Family were spoken of as instruments of use and power in Spirit hands, I could not myself see the propriety of their disdainful animadversions, and unhesitatingly concluded that their professed admiration for the truth and love for a more exalted world or kingdom of joy, righteousness and felicity—as announced in christian parlance—was but an accommodating fiction, better adapted to surrounding social life and general mental aptitude, than to meet and satisfy "that higher light of understanding," which finds its reward in "wise consideration" and unquestionable knowledge.

Thinking that I would like to hear the rappings I one day said to my mother, whose advice and approval I usually sought in the various acts and movements of my younger days:

"I guess, mother, I'll go out to Rochester ere long, and while there I'll make a visit to the Fox Family and listen to the "spirit noises." Perhaps I may receive a message or hear from Brother, especially if there's any truth in what people say."

"I think you'd better keep away from there, my boy," she smilingly replied, "the privilege of communing with spirits and angels is easier claimed than fulfilled, and moreover, if you go and listen to the sounds which are heard in the presence of the Fox girls, it will become known, and everybody in the neighborhood will laugh at you, and you'll be called a "devotee of the marvelous."

" Well," said I in reply, "if life is a battle to be
fought out, and the self-complacent indifference
of men is forever to obviate a claim to just and
honorable motives in the investigation of any and
every new subject, I am for once fully convinced
of my individual freedom of mind, and am ready to
meet in the contest of powers which is to decide the
fate of a generous sincerity on the one hand, or of a
bickering meanness and distrust on the other."

"I have not a wish in my heart, my boy," she
again remarked, "to interpose an objection to your
visiting the Spirits, but you know there are some
unhappy stories afloat concerning the family in
which the rappings occur, and those who go there
are usually made the butt of social jokes and pastime
at home."

"Yes," said I, "the privilege of abuse is however
only a negative assumption of the will. All free-
thinkers and reformers have been maligned, ill-treated
and ignored; the early christians themselves were kicked
and buffeted about by a presumptious and self-con-
ceited populace. They were sneared at and mortified
in their poverty. They wandered from place to
place and slept upon the bare earth; yet, notwithstanding these misfortunes and the hardships which
they endured, they triumphed in after generations,
and men bowed the knee in worshipful adoration
of the identical views and opinions which they had
so ignominiously contemned and scorned."

"The human mind is a wretched bundle of uncertainties," continued I, "and I confess a want
of respect for every characteristic of mental artifice

and deceit. It's not my pleasure, mother, to agree with those who *hope* rather than *know*, or who constantly forego the exercise of that desirable sincerity which is never out of place, and which the biggest fool in the world soon learns to respect when worthily associated in life."

My mother seeing that I was somewhat disturbed in that sense which I possessed of the proprieties and improprieties of human conduct and expressed sentimentality, very quietly answered:

"As for myself I don't think there's any particular harm in going to hear the "spirit rappings," but you know, "people will talk," and whether consistently or otherwise, the effect is about the same, for in the growth of public sentiment upon any subject error is quite as likely to be approved as truth, and whatever people think, whether right or wrong, is for the time being the strong belief which they most rely upon, and their sense of justice and conduct are mostly governed by this fortuitious conviction.

After a moments reflection I rather tartly remarked:

"I don't care much as to what people think. When I have a good opportunity I shall most surely go and hear the "rappings."

My mother smiled at my obstinacy, and with a most significent look replied:

"I guess you want to see the "Fox girls" more than you want to hear the sounds."

"Well," said I, somewhat distressed over her jocularity of mind, "you've got the better of me in argument this time." When with a hearty laugh at her merry expression our conversation ended.

In deliberating upon the subject of the "spiritual manifestations," I thought it not best to be in to great haste in arriving at conclusions, even though under the pressure of ample evidence. It was my determination however to regard the matter in the light of reason and candor whenever a favorable opportunity should offer, and to shrink no responsibility in my investigation of the phenomena through fear of popular objections or the opinions of others. The subject was new, and as my mother said, people would talk, but nevertheless as it was my habit to exercise the fullest freedom of mind upon every disirable occasion in life, I resolved to desist from no honorable purpose simply to satisfy the "stock-jobbers" in public sentiment, or to suit the more isolated and selfish interests of individuals who might have an ax of their own to grind.

The existence of spirit beings and their ability to demonstrate their presence was no longer a question in my judgment, and I believed those persons to be very illogical in their methods of reasoning, if not altogether unwise in their decisions, who could announce a propriety in refusing the examination of a subject so evidently important as spirit communion, or who would fly to the support of their "antiquated ideas" at a rate so expensive to the demands of knowledge.

Men, I remarked, seldom refused to handle gold because of the existence of its counterfeit; seldom refused to barter with degradation where a prospect

THE PHENOMENA OF SPIRITUALISM.

of gain was implied in the dealing, wherefore then, thought I, do they refuse to consider a subject, a phenomena of the most vital consequence? Are men in fear of the spirits of the death? Do they wisely avoid contact with their own departed kindred, Fathers, Mothers, Sisters and Brothers, made immortal through the very flesh and blood of their own households. Why is it that we are so peculiar? Have the spirit populations who have gone before, found an abiding place only in some proximate bedlam of the "invisible," that we dodge them as so many "malicious imps of darkness." If spirits are wicked men should know it. If good, they should make it a matter of happy consideration and pleasurable comment. John, the beloved apostle advised his followers, not to *renounce* but to "try the spirits," and thus determine whether they were good, and worthy of human confidence. What less can we do than acknowledge the wisdom of his advice, and benefit by his experience. His counsel was given, no doubt, as the result of observation and investigation. He had no fear of the dead, neither good or bad, but evidently desired to keep acceptable company in dealing with spirits, as he would in dealing with mortals.

It is unquestionable that due reflection will invariably suggest not only the propriety, but the absolute necessity of the exercise of a liberal, yet staid and unflinching criticism in the investigation of all new and difficult subjects; and it must ever be regarded as extremely unsafe to submit too willingly to a credence in matters which pertain to

the "mysterious," the "phenomenal" or the "unseen."
Indeed, it is quite certain that a just and legitimate
inquiry into any theory, subject, or philosophy, any
practical scheme in life, pursuit or purpose, can best
be made when the mind is on its guard as against
the encroachments of hasty and *accommodating* credulity.

In speaking of spirits we should ask ourselves
these questions: Why do they institute a system
of "physical manifestations?" Why do they at all
times cast a *veil of mystery* over their acts and
demonstrations? Why do they make themselves
known to some families and not to others? Why do
spirits approach us more frequently at night than
during the hours of day, and, especially, why do
they near us to cast their influences over mentality
and human consciousness in the twilight of the early
morning? Why do they impart unpleasant as well
as agreeable dreams and sensations? Why do they
often guide and direct individuals from harm ; then
again, as in other instances, molest the peace of a
whole community, or nation, by abusive processes in
psychologic "Obsession" and "Witchcraft?"

These and many similar inquiries must inevitably
arise in the mind of every investigator of the subject
of spiritual intercourse, and honest consideration
must ever suggest the necessity of the application
of every needful defense in criticism, ere the replies
received either through observation or accumulative
evidence, can be properly accepted and made a part
of our "better knowledge."

It is undoubtedly always justifiable to regard the

small or apparently insignificant facts and circumstances, which present themselves here and there in
new forms and phases for our reflection, as well as
the more important and prominent ones, for while
we may be satisfied in regard to the immortality
of the soul, and the possibility of spirit influence in
the actualization of various mortal interests, it is undoubtedly quite as true that without a general and
thorough comparison of existing facts, details or
minutia, the conditions upon which these essential
propositions depend, could not be so easily determined, and the intellect would thus remain unsatisfied, or in other words, the confidence of the mind
would rest in *belief* alone.

CHAPTER VII.

WENT TO HEAR THE RAPPING. REV. CHARLES HAMMOND. MOTIVES OF THE DEPARTED.

It was, dear reader, after long-continued desire,
and under the guidance of opinions, such as I have
herein freely presented, that in company with the

Reverend Charles Hammond, of Rochester, I visited the celebrated Fox Family, who were, as I have before written, then residing in that city. It was however several months subsequent to the receipt of the kindly advice which had been given me by my mother, and at a time when the interest felt in the subject of the "rappings" had become more intense and far more widely extended.

Mr. Hammond was occupying the desk of the Universalist Church in the village where I lived for a few sundays in the absence of the settled minister, who had been called away to some other locality to preach. Having been acquainted with my Father, who had formerly worn the clerical harness, but who had now divested himself of the cares and burdens which were implied in its use, he made it his pleasure on several accasions to stop at our house on the Sabbath day. It was during one of these visits that he extended a kindly invitation to my Father and his family to call upon him at his residence in the City of Rochester, promising at the same time that if we would do so, he would escort us, one or all, to the residence of Mrs. Fox, with whom he was well acquainted; that we might thus have the pleasure or satisfaction of listening to the "Spirit Rappings," and be thereby the better enabled to decide the question of truth or artifice, as employed in their production.

Mr. Hammond had become deeply interested, if not somewhat enthusiastic, in the investigation of the singular phenomena which had now taken the name of "Spiritualism," and which withall had made its appearance in other families than that of Mrs.

Fox, and in other localities than that of Rochester City. He had been accused by his brethren of the Universalist denomination, not only at home, but in other places, of mystifying, if not of almost wholly abandoning his relation with the Church. He was accused of teaching spiritualism in the pulpit, and was advised by his clerical associates not to permit a subject so demeaned in instability as "Spirit manifestations" to lead him from a faith in doctrinal christianity, or allow his personal interests to sink under a stigma so wretched, and which it was asserted would destroy every good prospect in his ministerial career.

Notwithstanding all this Charles Hammond made himself amenable only to the advice of his own heart and understanding, and fearlessly clipping his church record, entered the service of the Spirits Guides who first through the rappings, and subsequently through the mediumship of his own hand, adviced him in wise if not artful words to receive and cherish a mission in the confidence of spirit advice and counsel.

He unhesitatingly accepted the new situation which was thus offered, and without delay persued the convictions which he had formed during the first season in which he was engaged in the investigation of spiritualism.

Having some business of a personal nature to transact in the City of Rochester during the month of June, 1848, I visited that place, and while there called upon Mr. Hammond at his residence upon Sophia Street, where I was cordially received by himself and lady, and urgently requested to remain over night, to which invitation I accorded a most willing consent.

During the evening and while at his house it was my pleasure to listen to a recital of the details of the experience of Brother Hammond, as given in his own words, in regard to his examination of the strange phenomena of the mysterious noises. He related every particular as to how the rappings occurred, explaining wherein they differed from those sounds which, although in some manner similar, were produced by us; stating likewise that the spirits had manifested a singular inclination to a familiarity with himself, in answering his various questions, and in communicating with him by means of raps upon any and all occasions. He said also that they often touched his person, pulled his clothing, fumbled his hair, and during evening *seances* had frequently fanned his face with a picture which was painted upon canvass stretched over a frame, and which was taken from the place where it hung upon the wall, at Mrs. Fox's residence, and transferred by unseen hands a distance of twelve or fifteen feet for that purpose.

In his description of the scenes which he had witnessed he spoke of many wondrous tests which he had received from time to time from the "invisibles," and which he said were given to satisfy his mind concerning the future life and the truth of spiritual intercourse.

I listened to his narration of facts and particulars in regard to the doings of the spirits with emotions of surprise, and with feelings of the deepest concern and curiosity; and while I entertained many doubts

in regard to the matter I still cherished a hope
that his statements were not only true, but that in
the development of a system of orderly manifestations,
and without at once greatly interfering with the
more fixed opinions of men, the spirit world might
confer a happiness upon the human heart by bestow-
ing upon mankind some more direct and reliable knowledge concerning immortality, and the conditions of
life which such a state of existence necessarily implies.

Mr. Hammond seemed very much pleased with
his experience as an investigator of spiritualism, and
I really thought from his earnest manner of relating
his story, that I could observe an inclination in his
mind too zealous, if not over-hasty enthusiasm.

Prudence in reflection, thought I, as I retired to
my sleeping room that night, is a holy gift; to
detain our would-be desires, and those thoughts
which in their constant multiplication are too apt to
force us into premature convictions, if not hasty
action, is a purpose seldom adviced in human wisdom. The Rev. Charles Hammond is truly a
wondrous thinker, and is a man of marvelous ability
as a public speaker and orator. He chains his
audiences by an avalanche of words delivered in the
happiest flow of expression. Sometimes he wanders
in the realms of the imagination in discourse, and
seeming to forget his own effort, he succeeds in
binding the attention of his listeners by ideal figures
of speech and beautiful *impromptu* utterances. He is
a person who evinces the most unfaltering zeal and
determination in his efforts. Wherever his judgment
leads him—and his action in that is usually based

upon intuitive thought more than upon logical inference—there in unyielding, impolitic stubbornness,
stands this noble hearted and fearless advocate
of new ideas in religion and philosophy, whom his
enemies abuse in his goodness and magnanimity,
malign for his self-selection of thought, pure hope
in immortality and devotion to the interests of the
cause of spiritualism.

On the morning following my visit to Brother
Hammond's, and at about ten o'clock in the forenoon
we together through mutual desire and consent made
our way along several by-streets to the rather retired
and humble dwelling of Mrs. Fox. I was to have
an opportunity to hear the rappings and decide for
myself the question of disbelief or confidence. My
companion and guide was to introduce me at the
morning *seance*, and I was to take advantage of any
favorable moment or means to make inquiry of, or
communicate with the spirits. We approached the
house where the *Mediums* resided and rapping at the
door, were at once admitted, Mr. Hammond being
known and recognized as an acquaintance and friend
of the family, as well as an honest and earnest
investigator of the spiritual manifestations.

Passing through a narrow hall, to the right
of which was a small parlor, we ascended a short
flight of steps, and entering a small back room
which was elevated to accommodate the needs of a
kitchen below, we were invited to a seat beside a
large double-leafed dining table, where several persons
who were strangers, had already commenced to
organize a "circle for the sounds."

The room was without a carpet, and contained no furniture with the exception of a table, a half dozen chairs of ordinary pattern, and—if memory serves me—the addition of a somewhat well-worn lounge. I looked about, but saw nothing which indicated a desire on the part of the occupants of the house to practice deception upon visitors, or those who came to witness the spiritual demonstrations. The three sisters sat side by side at the table, while not less than seven other persons occupied seats around or near it.

As I sat in the circle listening to a familiar conversation which was going on concerning the various doings of the spirits—singular performances which were being every day enacted in the presence of the Fox girls—I could not help remarking the inimitable *sangfroid* which characterized their manners and appearance in the company of comers and goers, and which they evinced in their treatment of the manifestations of which they were the chosen instruments.

The two youngest girls were quite fair looking, if not handsome. The eldest sister, who was said to be married, was not less commended for the beauty of her features, and was. evidently the chosen ward who presided over the spiritual interests of the household.

As I looked at the young ladies seated in social chit-chat waiting the condescension of the spirits, I could not help thinking of the merry remark which my mother made about my being more interested in the "girls" than in the "rappings." I saw that they were pleasant and agreeable, as well as kind and obliging to all new-comers, and seeing no impropriety in their deportment, I concluded that at all events their acquaintance might not be less acceptable on account of their being attended by the "invisibles," or *wrapped* in mystery.

We patiently waited for something more than twenty minutes when suddenly and as if through concert of action a large number of soft and peculiar raps were produced apparently upon and under the table. These noises continued for some half hour or more, sometimes upon the floor, at others upon the ceiling above our heads, then again upon the side walls of the room and against the door which led to the hall without. A gentleman who was present and who seemed to be extremely scrupulous in regard to his notions about the sounds, asked permission to step into the hall to see if the spirits could produce the raps on the opposite side of the door.

His request was immediately granted, and the spirits rapped on both sides of the door at once with increased power and emphasis. He returned defeated. His chagrin and dissappointment were quite manifest as he re-entered the room and ejaculated:

"I guess there ain't any wire-pulling out there."

The alphabet was now called for and several words and sentences were spelled out for the benefit of those present. Mental questions were asked and answered. Mr. Hammond received a message of advice. A gentleman from Albion received replies to a number of inquiries, and expressed a thankfulness for what he had heard and seen. As for myself I sat like a monk, without words or favor from the unseen beings who presided over the demonstrations from the other world; yet I satisfied myself from observation that the *Mediums* were innocent as regarded the cause or origin of the mysterious noises; but as to whether they were *indispensable* vehicles for their production—as was commonly asserted—was to my mind an unsettled, if not a very doubtful question; for in view of the discreet intelligence which I observed was exercised by the spirits, and their ability to announce themselves by various unusual sounds at a considerable distance from the Misses Fox, I could see no just reason for thinking that the auric theory of their development was either true or reliable.

After an hour the *seance* ended, and although I had not personally communicated with any spirit, either mentally or orally, yet I was better pleased for having visited the Fox family in the freedom of my own mind, without fear, favor or prejudice; and while I was convinced that spirit rappings were a veritable truth, I saw that they were likewise a solemn riddle, too deep, too profoundly hidden in the knowledge of super-terrestrial minds to be easily understood; and I was equally as well adviced that the object of the manifestations was hampered and secreted in that wisdom which the "invisibles" alone possessed. That they desired to communicate with mortals was to clearly indicated in the evidences which I had witnessed to be denied, but that a *rule of restrictions operating under the ban of mystery* was

imposed upon the permission in spirit life to hold
converse with men, was also as certainly demonstrable from the ghostly maneuverings which I beheld,
or else the life of the "immortals" had become so
changed in its relation to earthly existence as to
upset every principle of order, law, or consistency as
known to us.

CHAPTER VIII.

VARIOUS OPINIONS CONCERNING THE DEPARTED.

As I returned home upon the conclusion of my
visit in Rochester, my mind inevitably reverted to
the spirits and the demonstrations which I had witnessed, and I reasoned with myself concerning them
on this wise: If the dead live, wherefore should
they remain silent or reticent of a disclosure of their
condition of existence. It is true that history furnishes
no case of common familiarity in intercourse with
the dwellers of another and a higher world, yet
many instances are known in which unseen in-

telligences have manifested their presence, and held conversational communion with men. Not less than forty remarkable cases of spiritual intercourse are recorded in the scriptures alone, while profane history abounds with unnumbered occurrances of a similar character, and with statements of unaccountable manifestations and events, which have come under human observation, as well to astonish and confound the wise, as to implant feelings of awe and superstition in the minds of the ignorant, the vulgar, and the unpretending. The legends of Ireland and Scotland abound in tales of ghost-seeing and revelations concerning the departed. The natives of the Nicobar Islands put up scare-crows around their villages to defeat and frighten away hostile and malicious spirits. The inhabitants of Kamtchatka complain of and insult the spirit deities of the air whenever their wishes are unfulfilled. The Jorubans of Africa believe that dreams are not the result of an irregular action of the brain, but are a product of spirit influence, and so many revelations from the beings of another sphere. The North American Indian never falters in the chase, nor ceases to hunt for his enemy, when inspired by that confidence which is based upon his dreams and the advice and counsel of the prophets. The Greenlanders believe in visions and think that at night they actually engage in hunting, visiting and courting.

Thus nearly all savages conceive of a life beyond the earth and believe that they are visited by the spirits of the dead. This instinctive idea pervades the records of every nation, and crops out

in the prevailing religious sentiment of every age.
Mind naturally seeks to know itself, and in a state
of ignorance belittles the object of its own desire, by
fictitious conceptions and false assumption in knowledge. The undeveloped intellect, it is true, is not
wholly amiss in its convictions concerning the unseen
and the eternal. It may be, in a degree, mistaken
through fear and false education, but there is a basis
of truth connected with the universal belief of man
in spirit life and visitation, or else all inference is
unreliable, all history uncertain, and human
ideas of truth abusive of the happiness of life, as
well as contradictory of the evident purposes expressed
in the "designs of nature."

The spirit rappings, thought I, as I reflected,
furnish incontrovertible proof of the existence of
spirit beings. Beings whom we cannot see, with
whom we cannot speak, save through processes
of their own adoption. The quibbles of "invisibles," the
contradictions of which many complain, are no
evidence against an established truth. Even the
doubts which are engendered and which men entertain from this seemingly unhappy cause, may yet
prove a judgment in the better interest of human
understanding. Mind is presumptious, assuming, staid,
self-satisfied and unintentionally willful. The desires
and feelings of the heart are not always in unison
of purpose with the decisions of the intellect or
the wisdom of the soul. There is a perpetual conflict
between joy and sorrow, passion and reason, and we
are ever short of knowing the extent of our own
intelligence or ability. Spirits may reach in knowl-

edge beyond our conceptions of the capacity of mind to comprehend. They may see it to our disadvantage to speak with us in freedom, "as a man speaketh with a man." The world has need of a demonstration of immortality perhaps, more than of the "sublime particulars" of a future life. Were this not so, intercourse with the dead would certainly have been granted centuries ago, and even now would not come hoodwinked by *mischief, mystery and rules of equivocation.*

Spirits must see mankind *exactly as they are,* and appoint their mission to correspond with their conceptions of our needs. Indeed, we may not be as worthy as we believe ourselves to be. The religious sects hold this communion with the departed to be objectionable; they are humiliated by its humble methods; they say it is truckling and undignified, and molests their established systems of faith and worship. Some say it cannot be true. That it is really false, degrading and mischievous, in this, seldom thinking of the fictions of the imagination upon which all theology is founded, and which doses the human mind with nostrums of thought, too sickening to be ever justified in reason where selfish motives and interests are ignored.

The spirits are vindicable in the course which they persue or else they are consumately hardhearted, indifferent to mortal affection, if not absolutely wicked, said I, as I deliberated upon the subject of what I had seen, heard and read concerning their recent maneuverings, and while I do not believe in the malevolent enmity which prompts abuse and personal slander, I conceive it to be just and right

that men should be wary, critical and discerning in
their investigation of a phenomena so astonishing
and unusual. People assult the private character
of mediums as an argument against a system of unaccountable manifestations. Of what consequence is the
private life of a family in view of the *actual* in a cause so
wondrous. Our inclination to haste in personal
accusation is a fault, yet it often seems to advance
a better judgment in the interest of truth. We cover
up our own defects and mistakes, and to serve a
selfishness in individual wants and understanding, we
cast stones with careless freedom. We revile and
annoy each other for those differences which should
be considered and reconciled. The peace of a nation
is always in jeopardy where ignorance dominates
in society, and men are in conflict of sentiment over
the plainest evidences of knowledge. Religious bigotry is the most terrible blunder of human confidence.
All our commutative relations are sordid and care-
worn as a consequence of our deceit, and illiberality
in considering subjects of interest. The whole world
is in a conflict of views over questions concerning
"equal rights," "general laws," "intelligence," "ecclesiastical authority" and "commercial relations." The
Japanese have heretofore refused foreigners permission
to settle in their 'Golden Empire," while the Americans
opened their doors and welcomed the world to partake
of their joys and hospitality. The extremes of rebuff are housed in every heart, and animadverted in
every bosom. Wherefore are we to chide spirits for
not conforming to *our* conceptions of right and

wrong? Let us welcome any testimony which is likely to satisfy us of the safety of our kindred in immortality. If death brings peace and wisdom as most religionists assert, then a judgment of angelhood is over us, and our worth as individuals and nations is measured with minutest accuracy, and our intercourse with the "heavenly hosts," is guaged to suit the value of our mistakes, pretences and inimical comprehensiveness of mind.

We must admit that spirits and angels are little improved by the change of death, when we become their dictators, and decide in what manner they may or may not communicate with us. Self-satisfaction in knowledge may be adopted as a panacea for righteousness; but mind is ever more happy, as well as more consistent, when it is willing to measure the entire circumference of being. Mankind are given to habits and opinions wholly local in their origin, and childishly exclusive in their application to practical life. The Chinese twist their hair into a tail, smoke opium in large quantities, and barter incense with Jos, the God of their adoration. The Arabs sport their red, white and gray turbans, invoke the name of the prophets, prostrate themselves within their mosques, and then, in conformity to habit, go out to mingle with men and overshadow all truth in human dealing, by equivocation, hypocrisy and foibles of the tongue. The Lapps put the images of their Gods into separate boxes, and write thereon their several names, that they may not get confused in regard to their

E

own identity. The Kyoungtha of Chittagong usually
worship morning and evening, beginning by ringing
a set of bells to inform Boodh, their principle Deity,
that they are in readiness to offer their prayers and
suplicate for mercy. The Kaffirs, when on a mar-
auding expedition, give utterance to various peculiar
cries and hisses, thinking thereby to deceive the
Divinities in regard to the objects of their pursuit.

O, consistency; blessed state of mental desire,
thou art truly too often abridged of thy holiness and
worth through folly and ignorance in human life.
Men worship God in a thousand ways; but why do
they so belittle the characteristics of his being in
seeking his kindness and compassion? Commodore
Perry asserts that in a Chinese Temple he saw an
image of the Devil represented in human form and
possessing a most hideous physiognomy, while in
front of him was placed the image of the virgin and
child. This was indeed a most anomalous assortment
of company, and was probably the result of a mis-
conception of christian customs, or of the application
of ideas to principles. The human mind abounds in
a strange admixture of sense and nonsense, and
those who presume to know the most, are often-
times the source of the greatest mistakes as well as
of the greatest misfortunes to themselves and others.
The *actual* in life, in nature, in thought, escapes their
recognition. They follow the pathway of a "fatherhood departed," and cling to the "old signs" and
"established habits," under the impulse of fear, hope,
desire, ambition and custom. They are not patient
in reflection, neither circumspect in observation; but

like the barnacle which clings to the ships bottom;
they hold on with unyielding force, if not satisfaction,
to the "hobby of life's earliest choice." The imagination is constantly drawn upon to furnish a substitute
for more substantial knowledge, comprehensiveness,
deliberation, discernment, and wise discretion are
surely wanting in every system of religion known to
humanity. The only thing which makes the christians faith more worthy, more acceptable than all
others, is its *pliability*, or recognition of the idea
of progress. In other words, its conformative
development as manifested under the pressure of the
advancing tide of intelligence and civilization. Mind
seeks for a knowledge of things which are hidden
and difficult to understand. It looks to the eternal
for satisfaction in being, but receiving the rebuff or
disappointment which ignorance usually confers upon
itself, it holds a counsel over its own ideas and conceptions, and finally chooses like the lost man in the
forest the best alternative. There is no wrong in
the influence which makes men and nations differ;
but the absence of wrong motives in the cause which
produces variability in things or ideas, is no evidence
of the presence of absolute truth, much less of the
exercise of justice toward men, as authorized in the
more acceptable ways of wisdom.

When spirits come to the earth they are either
good or bad. Who is to decide this important question? Is it those who remain at home and make no
effort, or those who "try the spirits?" Perhaps they
are all good, and more intelligent than we presume
them to be. May it not be possible that our own

defects, follies, and wickedness are the cause of the insecure manifestations which we receive? Perhaps our notions concerning human equality, justice and equity are not founded in righteousness. Perhaps we are not worthy of higher recognition from the spirit world. Would men feel happy to know that angels are far more humble than themselves, being greatly more wise. Our arrogance may be a punishment to us in heaven, and our self-centered charity and personal conceit may receive a just rebuke in sorrow when we least expect it. Give to the poor and needy, was the command which Christ gave to his followers. But the rule would seem to have been reversed in modern times, for the rich who claim to worship according to his teachings, not only struggle to increase their own wealth, but the labor of the poor is the foundation of their success.

If spirits are wicked, we should know it. If our kindred in immortality, our Fathers, Mothers, Sisters, Brothers, Aunts, Uncles, Cousins have degenerated, or have been denuded of common sense as a consequence of their transition to another condition of existence, then certainly it behooves us to make our stay upon earth as long as possible, nor should we yearn to know of a state of being which degrades our happiness, or bemeans our intelligence.

No, no; such opinions are as fictitious as the fleeting wind. We may mystify the honor, the goodness of the Divine Being by circumlocution in thought and expression, may barter away our joy and hope in a raid of words upon the godlessness of spirits, because they *rap* their notes of warning to the world, because they tip tables and make mock faces to establish the fact of their existence and prove their identity. We may chide God for making the Devil to torment his own kingdom and power, as men have too often done, but when we comprehend nature, when we know ourselves, and grasp the broad possessions of creation with the refined telescope of mind, our fictions vanish, our follies depart, our mistakes become corrected, our beliefs annulled, our opinions and convictions changed. We are no longer selfish, we hold no enmities, we seek no sorded satisfaction in life, we are humble, kind, unassuming, just and generous. Our religion becomes universal, our love all embracing. We have confidence conceived in sobriety, and happiness founded upon justice and virtue. The broad earth is our delightful home, the expansive heavens our pleasure. Study embracing the wondrously amplified features of creation becomes our joy, while the myths of past ages no longer thwart the objects of reason, nor intrude themselves upon the freedom of manly consideration.

Such were some of the many thoughts which brooded over my mind, immediately after my visit to the Fox Family, and during the long weeks and months of the years eighteen hundred fifty-one, two, three and four; and during all that time I was quietly engaged in the toilsome duties of domestic life, ploughing in the fields upon my Father's farm, hoeing corn, cutting and securing grass and grain, gathering fruit from the orchards near our dwelling, or caring for the meager stock which we

kept, during the cold blustering days of winter. I
had not forgotten the "Spirit Rappings." I sought
for the opinions of men concerning them. They
were unsatisfactory, often frivolous, and seldom profound. The subject was unpopular. People smiled
when the spirits were mentioned. The *savants* were
befogged. Feeling humiliated because unable to explain a mystery, they shrugged their shoulders and
expressed their indignation by the sobriquet of "humbug." I had but little to say about the "manifestations." My neighbor, said I, was a spiritualist, however, and "greatly beside myself in the adoption of
such a belief as that." Beards were then unpopular,
and I was laughed at for wearing a moustache and
beard, especially by the ladies. They said I looked
like an ape and was strangely constituted to be
fanatical in my views. The church people said that
I ought to let spiritualism alone. That I was a very
upright young man, paid my debts, was just and
honest, but that spiritualism was a *terrible thing.* I
loved them better for the short-sighted privilege
of abuse which they enjoyed and exercised over my
dependent circumstances in life, and I sought no
redress for the wrong which I sustained. I contemplated spiritualism with independence, with fearless-
ness, and a hope for its truth. I believed not in the
pretences of men. I was convinced of the utter
ignorance of all the world in regard to a future life.
The word heaven, it is true, was familiar to the ear,
and the immortality of the human soul was a theme
of thought often indulged in; but the demonstration
of a condition of existence beyond the earth, its

cause, its certainty, the why and the wherefore, belonged not to mortal man to explain.

In spirit communion I saw a hope, a practicle guarantee of the safety of the soul when the physical body was laid aside. I saw that the motives which actuated men were based upon selfish purposes. They had not so much objection to spirit rappings, as they had to a flurry over certain fixed opinions of their own views not necessarily sincere, but usually appointed in self-interest and founded upon educational precedent. My mind was free from all religious bias, and I concluded to do my own thinking. I loved my father who was an old man. He had been a theologian, was a thinker, and under the inscrutable influence of thought had adopted the freest sentiments of mind. People said he was insane upon the subject of spiritualism. Nay; his body was worn out. His brain was in the decay consequent upon old age, and his thoughts were therefore rendered in a somewhat garbled expression. He was near the grave. His belief in sectarianism was damaged. He saw through its films, and no longer courted its recognition. He had no objection to the worship of the heart in whatever form, but he ignored the idea of *accommodation* in religion. He was maligned, slandered and mostly confined at home in self-selection of life during the ten long years which closed his earthly career.

I say, I loved my Father, for he penetrated the shams of ecclesiastical lore and logic, and stood upon the broad platform of knowledge or nothing. He was too old to investigate the phenomena of spiritualism with any degree of accuracy or wisdom, but he cherished the strongest hope that its claims might become established; that communion with the departed might be realized. He was nearing the home of the everlasting world. Four out of six of his children had already passed over the river of death. They were spirits. They were his children, and he still cherished a hope in their goodness and a desire in their interest. Were his wishes amiss? Those who knew him best knew him to be good, kind and strictly honest. But they said, "his belief in spirits is a *great mistake*." He should go to church, and hear the Rev. Axumoff's sermon on the "purity of the angels, and the devil's wicked work."

CHAPTER IX.

FURTHER REFLECTIONS. FREE THINKERS. BEAUTY OF NATURE. A STRANGE SIGHT.

Mind is a most singular admixture of doubts and certainties, of satisfaction and dissatisfaction, of joy and sorrow, of belief and disbelief, of self-abnegation and arrogance, of pride and humility, of devotion, distrust, querulousness and irregularity. The differences which men manifest in their ideas, in their actions, in appearance, and in their inclinations, are too little considered, hence to objectionably regarded.   Our unwillingness to conciliate the opinions of others, our desire to foist our individual views upon the world and our refusal to acknowledge the blessing of adverse thought, is a mark of individual' fogyism and pusillanimity which demonstrates the existence of bigotry, and proves the insecurity of the intelligence which we posses.   Every person should *identify* his or her peculiar views, and should be permitted to give expression to the sentiments of the heart and understanding.   It is the purpose of nature that we should differ, that our differences should augment our knowledge and serve to establish our wisdom upon that permanent basis which is rigidly cautious, yet amply willing, nobly generous, and highly just.   In the social and intellectual commerce of life we are all liable to commit mistakes, to make blunders, to plunge into misfortunes, hopelessness and despair.   But experience is the winner, and the individual most annoyed, most studious, most worthy, like the pebble most worn, will present the most exact as well as the most polished characteristics. The many trials and difficulties which he encounters, the many obstacles which he has to overcome, the suffering which he endures, all tend to awaken his thoughts, improve his judgment, refine his manners, and exalt his nature to conditions of greater perfection and harmony.

Not long subsequent to my visit with the Rev.
Charles Hammond, at his residence in the City
of Rochester, my attention was called to an examination of the claims put forth in favor of the teachings
of the Harmonial Philosophy by several eminent and
able writers, men of profound thought and of great
ability, eminent alike as scholars and authors, the
friends of humanity, and the agents and advocates
of the most liberal opinions.   Among these were
Andrew Jackson Davis, the seer, The Rev. R. P.
Ambler, Appollos Munn, Rev. S. B. Brittan, Judge
John W. Edmonds, Hon. Nathan P. Falmage, Robert
Dale Owen, Robert Hare, the practicle chemist, and
many others who were equally as earnest in their
investigation of the "mysterious manifestations"—which
were then attracting public attention in many portions of the country—as they were honest, sincere
and deserving as expounders of this, and the "new
philosophy" which received its origin therefrom.

Through the various efforts which were made by
these distinguished theologians, scientists and thinkers, much was accomplished toward supplying the
many needed explanations and arguments upon the
subject of spiritual intercourse and phenomena, which
as a result of prevailing incredulity, yet of constantly
awakening desire among the people were really so
much demanded.

Mr. Davis, the inoculate author, confounded the
sentiments of a nation by his marvelous extemporaneous utterances and exhibition of unstudied knowledge. His inspirations were the most wondrous event
of the age. His mind reached the loftiest conceptions

in theoretical and philosophical thought, and his logic stood the test of the strongest scrutiny.

The Rev. R. P. Ambler was the first lecturer upon the subject of the spiritual phenomena, became the guardian of the "Spirit Messenger," and fearlessly met the opposition of the world.

The Rev. S. B. Brittan published the "Spiritual Telegraph," received the various opinions of writers and correspondents, and together with his own views, which were always clear, concisely stated and well applied to existing needs and demands, sent them forth to bless a hope in human life.

Judge Edmonds took the newly imported demonstrations into his household, and bartering no honor, labored with candor and becoming zeal to aid humanity to a better understanding of the "life beyond."

Dr. Hare tried the spirits by many scientific methods, giving them very little spare time for jocularity or unmannerly exhibitions of their presence and power. Indeed, he confined them to the rigid rules of chemical and mathematical demonstration, and proved their existence independent of mediumistic contact.

The Hon. N. P. Talmadge, Warren Chase and Robert Dale Owen saw and accepted the new light and aided in the decimination of its vivifying influence by every possible effort to humanity. They sent their thoughts abroad over the earth to sanctify the opening of communion with the immortal world, and to convince mankind that the judgments of heaven were awarded to men.

These were some of the tried and true souls,

who undauntingly, yet in the face of numerous objections, obstacles and discouragements, struggled to
establish the important fact of the agency of spirits
in the production of the modern "mysterious developments." They aided the cause of liberal thought by
numerous well-timed arguments, statements of facts,
and by well-expressed opinions upon subjects of liberal
interest, both orally and in writing. Their ideas and
sentiments were embodied in the literature of the
times, and together with those enunciated by others
—able thinkers and considerationists, both in Europe
and America—tended to win confidence, secure respect, and demonstrate the practical benefit to be derived from a comparison of views upon the subject
of communion with another and a higher world.

In the midst of the ever accumulating duties
which pertained to the accommodation of a household, being left to shoulder the cares and responsibilities which were placed to my account as a consequence of the decrepitude of an aged Father, who
was no longer able to properly attend to his own
business affairs, I was temporarily debarred from the
happy privilege of continuing my investigation
of the phenomena of spiritualism, and for some time
I gave but little heed to the many strange evidences,
singular manifestations and new phases of mediumship, which presented themselves here and there in
various parts of the country, as well to amuse the
frivolous and inconfident as to confound the thoughtful and the wise.

The direction given to my thoughts in childhood,
however, and the interior causes which prompted my

mind to the contemplation of things "spiritual," were nevertheless silently in active process of being continued, to the furtherance of personal satisfaction in the acquisition of a knowledge of the truth of the immortality of the human soul, the nature of the laws of mind, and the conditions of life as likely to be experienced by the released spirit.

Ever and ever the spontaneous desire for such knowledge increased. The great problem of mankind's existence and destiny worried my thoughts and discomposed my soberest reflections. The real joy of life was broken, and the nobler purposes of manhood lagged through indifference caused by the despair of the heart over the defective comprehension of the intellect in its grasp for the great "hereafter."

I went out upon the hills; I wandered alone in the woods; I stood beside the purling stream; I listened to the merry birds as they delivered their sweet notes of melody in inadvestant self-contentment of being; I sat down upon the gray moss beside a broad-armed green-clad hickory tree and mused in sorrowful despondency.

I had read theories and considered philosophy. My Father had been a teacher of theology. The benefit of his reflections had been mine to enjoy. I had heard the "spirit rappings;" had thoughtfully regarded the writings of A. J. Davis; had perused some of the writings of Swedenborg; was somewhat familiar with the scriptures; had experienced many singular realizations in life, although quite young, and had enjoyed much personal happiness as a result of observation and the opinions which I had formed concerning man, nature, freedom, justice, and the sublime power and influence of the Divine Mind: still I was not satisfied—I was yet seeking.

The spirit *demiza* was interestingly mysterious, and more than mysteriously interesting. I could not comprehend the usefulness of *deceit*, neither the need of restrictions upon social commerce with the "immortals."

"Providing spiritualism is true," I reflected, "and of that there can be no doubt—why do the spirits contradict themselves? Why do they bicker over thought and nullify each other's statements by circumlocution and ambignity in expression? Why amuse themselves at our expense, yet claim to possess and enjoy the most exalted happiness and wisdom."

Their messages are many times as well worthy of the head as heart, then again they are nonsensical, trashy, malignant, shallow, *wordy*, and unworthy of the attention of sincere and thoughtful persons. Their answers to questions are many times straight-forward, well-conceived, honest, reliable, and perfectly satisfactory. Then again they are uncertain, confused, of doubtful signification, if not over-adviced and meddlesome.

"Mankind," thought I, as I looked up into the pure blue ocean of space far above the forest trees which grew in stately majesty upon the hill-sides near where I was resting, "are more *presumptious* than *knowing*; are more given to the *pursuit* of knowledge, than to its *acquisition*. They say spirits are this, and spirits are that. They theorize, and philosophize, hectorize and dogmatize, confound their own logic and part company with common sense."

The more I considered the subject of a future life, the more I realized that man possessed no *positive* knowledge concerning it. That his prospects in eternity were only happyfied, so to speak, by "Faith," "Hope," "Inference," "Confidence," and that ambiguousness of thought which ensconces itself in a sea of words without critical analysis of their meaning or contents. The *belief* of the christian I considered not unworthy, but his *practice* of the precepts advocated by the teachers of his choice, proved contradictory of the sentiments advanced and the belief professed.

Thus I could find no consolation in uncertainty, in mystery, in doubts, confusion, equivocation or hypocrisy. I went out to nature in my deep, deep heart, and confessing my own ignorance and impotence of being, I consoled myself in sadness as I gazed upon the beautiful creations which surrounded me. The hemlock stood over by the water, casting its dark shade into its bosom. The branches of the yellowish-foliaged chestnut hung downward, heavily laden with full clusters of fruit-bearing burs. The white oaks with their long arms clothed in nature's garb of leaves, and producing abundance of acorns, shaded the rolling earth in every direction. The maples with their dense green foliage and admirable forms addressed the sense of sight with pleasure. A cluster of flowers with variagated hues grew beside the little brook, and the honey-bees were buisily engaged among them securing their sweets. A brown wren flew from her nest within a confused mass of stumps, logs and brush, and dancing upon a twig quickly darted from my sight. A song-thrush mocked the elements of music by the throttle of his tongue under the bushes hard by. The shrill whistle of the Woodchuck sounded upon my ear from the slope of a hill to my right. All nature was busy. The waters babbled along through the valley. The leaves of the silver *Pioppo* were restless in the breeze. A flurry of wind moaned through the trees. Again I looked heavenward. I thought of my sisters who were dead, of the Brother whom I had loved, and who was also now a spirit.

In nature I found *satisfaction*, in the sky *hope*.

God, the Universal Father, spoke in accents unmistakable in my soul. In everything which I beheld I saw evidences of the nearness and wisdom of the Divine Mind. The grass which lay beneath my feet was soft, green, beautiful and full of life; the forest grew in every leaf and limb. The running stream ceased not its monotonous song of joy either night or day. The bland breezes coursed along over the ridges and through every nook and dell, flouting here, softening there, maddening under the influence of pressure while passing through some narrow gulch, or mellowing down into zephyic mildness over the broad open plain.

The sun was sinking in the horizon of the West as I turned my footsteps toward home. I felt happier. I had communed with God in nature. *I found repose of mind in the works of the Creator.*

As I wandered homeward from the lonely retreat in the woods, where I had been for several hours, I turned my thoughts to the subject of the "After Life," and reflected concerning the probabilities of its being *actualized* in individual experience, knowledge, consciousness and identity in immortal realms.

"If the Spirit lives," said I, "it must have a place of abode. If it lives, it must possess the functions and qualities, in some measure, characteristic of beings of organized life. For nothing short of the organic form, in qualification, is endowed with power and ability to produce, or induce mental action, special manifestations of force, intelligence or thought. The wordy minister refers to "heaven" and "futurity," without definiteness or specialization, and the abode of the so called "wicked" remains · equally a place without a situation, location or position."

Thus I mused as I walked along. It was a peculiarity of my mind to seek consolation and happiness in the pursuit of reflection concerning the "great hereafter." Whether this sense was a result derived from an unseen psychologic impartation of desire, or was provoked as a consequence of an inherited inclination, I was unable to decide. I could not divest myself of the conviction however, that my deceased Sisters, Brothers, Relatives and Friends were still living. But *where*, was the unsettled question.

I strode along through the fields and over the fences, contemplating nature, and holding a silent Parle of words in my mind over the convictions of my own understanding, when ascending a rise

of ground which brought me in view of my Father's
house.   I paused for a few moments to rest from
my wearyness, seating myself upon the trunk of a
fallen oak by which I had to pass.   As I sat in contentment gazing upon the soft mellow light of the
declining sun which had now robed itself in the
splendors of the evening hour, I suddenly caught
the glimpse of a *restless shadowy something* in motion
in the air not more than twenty feet in front of my
position, and about as many from the ground.   I
fixed my eyes in closest attention upon the spot
where I observed the singular movement.   It appeared like a person swinging his arms in rapid evolutions.
I sank back in half-conscious despair and fright as I
saw the outlines of a transparent human figure.   It
was hardly discernible.   A fleece of light impressed
my vision for a single moment, and *all was gone.*

Amazed at what I had seen photographed amid
the elements of the atmosphere so near me, overwhelmed with astonishment and confounded in
understanding, I went home at last with a drooping
heart and heavy thought.   I was completely subdued
in mind.   I was distressed for want of knowledge.
My intellect was inadequate to the task of solving a
problem in philosophy—the problem of the appearance of "spectral forms."   I went to my books—a
meager supply—but could find no worthy solution
of the mystery.   A small volume entitled the "night
side of nature" written by Catherine Crow, and
compiled from unquestionable historic data, gave me
the gist of a new theme of thought.   Numerous
instances of similar waking visions were therein

related, but no satisfactory theory was adduced in
explanation of their cause or origin.   I was baffled.
The principles involved in their production, as in all
spiritual phenomena, were too profound, too deeply
hidden for ordinary discernment or comprehension.
I felt outwitted.   Nature was my master.   Out-
wardly I could discern her methods, her motions,
and active tendencies.   Her analogies were just,
reliable and conclusive.   But the spiritual elements
and motive principles governing matter were inscrutable.   I could not reach a knowledge of the system
of interior laws which were instrumental in the
production of such a manifestation as I had witnessed.

   "If it was an actual "spirit presence," I reflected,
"then the scene must be considered as so much the
more marvelous.   If it was a result substantiated
through the control of atmospheric ethers, or was
but a retinal impression enstamped upon my vision
by psychologic processes only known to beings
of another world, or if indeed it were but an "illu-
sion," supplanting the natural action of my mind—
in either case I can only regard it as a most singular presentation, and my desire to understand its
nature and cause, instead of being diminished, is
greatly increased.   I am therefore resolved to seek and
search with earnestness for the information which I
so much desire to possess, and which shall cancel
my ignorance—for it is nothing else—upon a subject
so extremely interesting and important."

   Concerning spiritualism, which still continued to
make rapid advancement and progress, and which

was being constantly re-enforced by accessions of new *Media* and new phases of manifestation, I was as well convinced of its truth as I was better satisfied that certain obstacles or hinderances were, through the design or wisdom of the invisibles, interposed to prevent that familiarity in intercourse with them, which the human heart and intellect in their natural inclination must so inevitably yearned to establish. I saw that spirits were accused of lying, of contradicting each others messages, of engaging in frivolity as a pastime for themselves and investigators. The fault finding and nicely proprietitious religionists, intimated that his barbe-tailed and behoofed majesty with the *proto-impcean* host, had introduced "raps" and "table-tipping" to deceive and mislead mankind. Then again some said it was *all a farce*, while others—the majority—*said nothing*.

For weeks and months I meditated. I believed but little. I sought to know more. I convened my own mental faculties, and privately debated every question of interest. The phenomena of spiritual intercourse was my joy, but I was not always pleased with the doings of the spirits. Their methods were not —according to my judgment—always to be approved, but of the correctness of the decisions of my own mind I gave room for many doubts. I presumed the angel world to be able to measure the needs of men and nations in all matters pertaining to the "great hereafter," and I confidently hoped for the best.

CHAPTER X.

PERSONAL REALIZATIONS. A VISION.

I have said, dear reader, that dreams and visions of a strange and impressive nature were, with me, a matter of common occurrance in my younger days. As I advanced in years these became facts of still more frequent experience, and sometimes were so remarkable in their varied characteristics, that the enigma of their singular features and design was as marvelous and unaccountable as it was many times a source of interest to consider. Sometimes my *interior* realizations were in every sense so like my inherent inclinations, so exactly a counterpart to the outward daily activities of my mind in thought, desire and observation, that I could hardly distinguish between that consciousness which was of dream-life, and that of wakeful self-recognition.

I was satisfied that mind possessed no ability in the absence of reflection and self-knowledge—as during sleep—to organize beautiful scenes, concoct plans, carry forward projects and purposes, travel, converse with friends and strangers, extemporize prose and poetry, get into unpleasant difficulties and become extricated by struggles, artful dodging and deceitful maneuvers, without extraneous aid. From reasoning I became fully convinced that spirits, our own departed kindred, were instrumental in the production of our dreams, and that the law of psychology was the basis upon which rested the holy privileges, as well as the unhappy experience, in them realized.

In the matter of my own convictions concerning this and kindred subjects I usually remained very quiet, seldom expressing an opinion in defense or even in reference to my own views, I was, it is true, often laughed at and objected to an account of my *belief* in spiritualism, which in verity was too often mistakenly magnified and misrepresented, as well through prejudice and thoughtless inadvertency of mind, as through studied malevolence, malice and design. It was owing to these facts that I prudently avoided any frequent allusion to the prevailing spirit manifestations, and those characteristic, mysterious laws of psychologic mental control, which were to me the greatest mystery in nature.

Thus I enjoyed the satisfaction of thinking privately and quietly, that my semi-trance realizations were prompted and produced—at least in a great measure—through the influence of invisible, intelligent beings. That they were often a source of much joy and comfort, I can certainly and most solemnly attest; for the *inward* eventfulness of the long night hours, which came freighted with scenes of happy significance and sublime beauty, often afforded subjects for the most delightful meditation, and gave relief to the mind in its otherwise monotonous habits of thinking.

I was the subject of strange impulses. Sensations and emotions, quite as annoying at times, as at others they were pleasant and agreeable, impelled me during daylight hours to the adoption of a choice in all things which pertained to the rotine of my personal duties and obligations in life; while, to use the phraseology of Scripture, I was, during sleep, often "caught up," and in visions of incipient clairvoyance boyantly floated heavenward, where being sustained by a seeming effort of my own will, I realized an amplification of experience by hundreds of miles of atmospheric journeyings. High above forests, cities and villages, over broad fields, plains and shining waters, with ease, comfort and happiness, I moved onward like a bird of passage, gazing upon herds and flocks which were grazing in finely cultivated fields in every direction, or looking down upon multitudes of people, who were going hither and thither to suit the diversified purposes which were constantly presenting themselves in the pursuit of life, as a result of individual enterprise, activity and interest.

Upon one accasion, which I still remember with the greatest pleasure, I took to flight, so to speak, in this manner from the earth and mounting the atmosphere to the very verge of the clouds, was rapidly conveyed over a wide extent of country which was decorated here and there with rolling hills,

green valleys, pure and beautiful lakes and still flowing rivers. I felt somewhat uneasy, as I passed
along with rapid flight far toward the eastward from
the place from which I had departed, I realized the
same inclination to a downward tendency, which I
had many times previously experienced. And it
seemed to be upon the strength of the effort of my
own will, that I was enabled to support myself and
journey along amid the congenial elements of the
moving stratums of the air. I could see many miles
toward every point of the compass. In the distance
to my right arose a range of lofty shattered mountains, lifting their bare peaks to the very heavens.
In the opposite direction and almost beneath my
feet, I beheld the sparkling waters of an ocean
whose smooth surface extended far beyond the ken
of vision. As I gazed downward, and far in advance
of my position I discerned the exterior line of an
arid desert. Quickly I neared the uninviting scene
with its broad stretch of parched sands looming upon
my sight. Not a tree, shrub, plant, flower or spear
of grass grew upon its face.

I now saw that I was floating amid the aereal
ethers, above a heated, yellowish, untilled solitude,
which was void of every living thing, and which,
from its unproductive and uninhabited condition, presented a hopeless and forlorn appearance, and sent a
thrill of sorrow to my already anxious heart. The
beautiful vales which I had seen, with their limpid
streams trailing along through the wood-lands and
open meadows, the flocks seeking shelter from the
sun beneath the shade trees in a thousand fields,

the orchards, the waiving grain, the presence and industry of man, were no where to be observed.

I felt lonely in my situation. A feeling of sadness and despair seemed to gain access to the sensibilities of my soul. As I advanced in my super-terrestrial flight, I observed that I began to loose that boyancy of being, which I had kept up by the effort of my will, and which I had almost inadvertantly exercised. I noticed, also, that I began to descend toward the barren waste below me, while yet struggling mentally to buoy up my floating form. As I looked to the eastward while making a gradual descent to the earth from my exalted position, I discovered, many miles in front and to the left of my location, a silvery sheet of shining water. This was margined by low-lands covered with dense vegetation and forest trees, which reached back to the line of the barren sands of the desert. Upon turning my face to the south-east, I noticed upon an elevated point of the arid plain not far away a grand old temple of massive masonry, which covered a wide area of sandy soil, and was standing entirely alone, unoccupied and apparently deserted. The greyish-yellow sand had drifted up against its western walls, and lay in great ridges, extending from its extreme sides many rods in opposite directions.

I felt attracted to this solemn and majestic work of art, and could not restrain the inclination of my mind to view its interior. I at once lost my ability to continue a wondrous aereal journey. My *will* failed to hold my body up, and I quickly descended to the entrance of the temple upon its southern wing.

F

Mounting a broad piazza or portico which was covered by a wide arch and supported by large stone
columns of greyish marble, and which from their
time-worn and frastured condition gave positive
evidence of great age, I entered a door which led to
a most spacious apartment, and one which I judged
from appearance had once been used for purposes
of religious worship, as a hall for public speaking, or
some similar use.   The room was empty with the
exception of an elevated platform at one end, a large
pile of mixed and cast off rubbish in one corner, and
a broken image which leaned back in a grotto in
the rear of the rostrum giving diversity as well as a
lonely look to the scene.

Observing a wide opening or entrance to a hall
in one corner of the room, I at once directed my
footsteps thither.   Pursuing the avenue to its termi-
nation, and turning to my right, I found a door
which opened into another apartment, not as commodious as the first, but far more elegant and
inviting in consequence of its varied architectural
decorations. I gazed upon its central concave arches
with a feeling of delight.   Its high wrought and
beautifully grottoed cornice, embellished with scrolls
of a most ingenious and attractive form, with here
and there images hanging in alto-*relievo* from the
walls, and diversified by colors inwraught, intermixed
and transposed in every part, lent an appearance
of grandeur, and a charm to the scene which completely overcome my mind, and I sat down all alone
in silence to enjoy rest and meditation.   I was
transported with delight, every object pleased my

sight. It was a vacant court of magnificent design and elaborate finish, wherein a people of primeval origin had met to worship in the love of nature. Nothing could exceed its fading splendor. As I arose from my seat and was directing my footsteps toward a narrow flight of stairs which I had observed in an angle of the room, I suddenly espied upon the wall near me, the following sentiment, which seemed to rise in beautiful golden letters from its surface:

TIME, THE BUILDER.
TIME, THE DESTROYER.
WAS. IS. IS NOT.

As I observed these words, my vision ended. I awoke, and instead of finding myself in a grand old temple, where it seemed to me as though I was actually gazing upon the gorgeous beauty and stately grandeur of the architecture of departed ages, I found myself snugly laid away in my bed at night, and surrounded by the most impenetrable darkness.

What a change! A complete mental revolution. An exaltation of the senses. The Mind, the Spirit, lifted up and enraptured by a most definite abnormal experience. My thoughts were perplexed, my reason was confounded, yet I was not without satisfaction in what I had seen and realized. But what was the cause of such a vivid dream? Certainly, thought I, the mind possesses no interest in things or scenes which it never conceived of. It is more reasonable to believe that such impressions are the result of "angel ministration," or of "spirit influence," than of inherent, individual inclination, as established in

the independent action of the intellect. Nothing
short of a foreign control of the mental faculties
could ever produce a vision so perfect to the realization of every sense of the soul. The mind has no
capacity to reach out in thoughtful consciousness and
the enjoyment of felicitious visions during the hours
of sleep, without the aid of some extraneous, intelligent cause. There is no truth, or propriety in the
supposition that the spirit is capable of *wandering in
dreams*, or that the mind may accommodate itself by
special action wholly unsolicited, as in observation
unexpected, in research unsought, in laborious journeyings, in flights, in trials, difficulties and sufferings,
during moments of slumber, without the intervention
of psychologic laws. The mind is an instrument,
and when at rest, may be acted upon in its various
faculties and functions by unseen powers. The Guardian Watcher may attune the latent elements of the
soul to an expression of the most happy and harmonious conceptions, perceptions and actualizations.
There is no *wandering in dreams.* The sense of seeing,
of hearing, of taste, of touch, of smell, as experienced
in the abnormal state of sleep, of somnambulism,
of trance, are wholly confined to superinduced action
within the limit of the *encephalon.* The spirit is not
released from its confines within the complex nerves
of the senses. The organic form of the soul is fixed,
established, permanent, and cannot be changed;
neither can the spirit be free from its *habitat* within
the structures of the physical body and brain, short
of death. But the mind once calm, quiet, happy and
tranquilized in natural and peaceful sleep, may re-

ceive the imposed sensations, impulses, feelings and inclinations which are imparted to it, or cast upon it from heights and distances undetermined, by the will-effort of the unseen monitionists of the heavenly household.

The more we each consider the subject of our own *interior* experience, the better satisfied we became of the fact that the same rule, law, or principle —that of mystery—governing the production and introduction of dreams and visions to the senses of the slumbering soul, is identical with that controlling the physical manifestations, and development of spirit power, as given through the rappings, in table-moving, and the twenty or thirty other known forms of mediumship. But why the existence of this law or principle of amplification and confusion in dreams and spiritualism? We are conscious that dreaming is a universal privilege and is enjoyed by nearly every living person. That of any community of one thousand people, not less than a quarter of the whole number, awake from their slumbers each morning to announce the felicity or infelicity of their abnormal impressions.

The indefiniteness, the *mystery*, the strange inaccuracy and inconsistency, the singular admixture of ideas and scenes, and the unlooked for operations and performances which pertain to dreaming and the state of sleep with their kindred conditions of trance, extasis and somnambulism, furnish an enigma as well to deep for ready comprehension, as it is justly calculated to afford food for mental reflection, deliberation and remark.

Not a household thought I, is without its Spirit
Watchers. Even the poor, the humble, the unworthy,
the vicious, the degraded and the wicked, have
friends who have died. They are no less the guar-
dians of earthly populations than the opulent, the
aristocratic, the educated and the wise. We all love
our own relatives and pride ourselves upon our
chosen associates. It is easy to fix a fate for others,
but it were wiser to seek to know of our own.
If our deceased kindred live, they have not abandoned the deep, fixed and abiding friendships and
loving regard, built up and supported in family
domestication, and neighborly intercourse. They are
still our kindred, our Brothers and Sisters, Fathers
and Mothers, and through the success of Divine law
as substantiated in nature, they are permitted or
enabled to live near us unseen and unknown. We
entertain suspicions of their presence, intimations
of their nearness, and declarations of their continued
life and love. Dreaming is but one of their happy
hints, one of their kindly yet obscure suggestions,
of acquaintanceship, memory, consideration, attachment, favor, affinity, recognition or salutation.

But still it is asked why are dreams so peculiar.
Some are prophetic and reliable, others are wise
and wondrous. Some are beautiful and full of joyous
happiness to the dreamer, while the majority are
strangely compounded of sense and nonsense, of conceptions received in order and disorder. People are
often saved from harm or led into conditions
of prosperity and happiness through a belief in
advisory dreams. Some are made anxious, others

suspectful; some feel unsettled, or hold a doubt, a fear, a hope, a prejudice from the same cause. All are more or less blessed by the process of dreaming. No one was ever known to be harmed thereby, however much they may have *seemed* to suffer therein.

These were some of the many thoughts which arose in my mind from time to time as a consequence of my individual realizations as a visionist and dreamer. As to the correctness of my impressions or views upon this subject, the reader will be better able to decide perhaps after considering what may be offered concerning it in still other pages of this volume.

CHAPTER XI.

A YEAR'S TRAVEL. STRANGE PHENOMENA IN SPRINGFIELD, ILLINOIS.

Owing to the needs of my family, and the necessity of my providing for their support, I entered into an engagement in the Spring of 1856 to travel in the West with a theatrical company under the managcment of my brother-in-law, Mr. G. A. Hough, a gentleman ever respected by the "members of the profession," and Mr. Samuel Myers of Chicago, son-in-law of the once famous Dan Marble.

My wife had followed the calling of an actress and *danseuse* during four years previous to our marriage, but preferring the quiet and comfort of private or home life, and following the duties and obligations which were imposed upon her as a result of my circumstances and desires, she had not at the time here referred to appeared upon the stage more than once or twice during several seasons.

Our journey to the West was rather unexpected. My brother-in-law had been to New York to engage people for his company. Upon his return he called at our house to make a brief visit as had long been his custom. While with us, he solicited our services, which after due reflection and a mutual understanding as to what salary we were to receive, and *et cetera*, we concluded to grant as well to his command as interest.

In a few days we had made all necessary preparation for a summer's travel. I had no desire *myself* to leave home at the time, to live a wandering and unsettled life, as my Father and Mother were both becoming considerably advanced in years, and needed my presence to look after their interests and enjoyments. But I was poor. My Father's scanty means were no more than sufficient for the maintainance of himself and wife, much less those of my own family, my sister and several grand children, together with friends and relatives, comers and goers, who are always necessarily entitled to receive our sympathies and favor in the bestowment of worthy accommodation and comfort. Hence as a matter of money alone I was induced to accept the engagement offered by Mr. Hough to myself and wife, and in less than eight days from the time of his visit to our house we were on our journey to the City of Dubuque, Iowa, where the various other members of the company were to meet for organization and the commencement of professional duties.

We arrived at Dubuque on the twenty-fifth day of April and remained there for something better than two weeks. From thence we journeyed to St. Paul, Minnesota, by steamer, where we remained nearly four months, returning in August by way of the Mississippi to Lyons and Davenport in the State of Iowa, and thence to Ottawa, Bloomington and Springfield, Illinois, during the fall and winter months.

It had early been determined by the managers of our troupe, which was composed of some twenty-five persons, that they would remain in Springfield during the session of the Legislature which was to convene in the month of December, as it was thought that the assembling of that body, if nothing more, would tend to render a theatrical season of three or four months not only pleasant, but remunerative to all concerned.

Upon arrriving at the capital of the State of Illinois on the twenty-second day of December, I found it somewhat difficult to secure a boarding place that would not absorb the weekly salary

of myself and wife, which at that time amounted to
the very acceptable sum of twenty-two dollars a
week.   After spending some three days looking about
here and there, during which time we were at a
hotel paying for day-board at a high rate, I had the
good fortune—as I thought—through the advice of a
friend to serve myself with a very comfortable room
in a somewhat retired inn which was near what was
then called Metropolitan Hall, where our performances were nightly given.   We entered our new
lodgings with pleasure.   The apartment assigned
to our use, was on the ground floor, was commodious and well furnished, but from the fact
that the windows were very small, and opened upon
a back yard, which was surrounded by high buildings
and which in a measure shut out the light, it wore
a gloomy appearance, which was not only remarked
by my wife, but by nearly every one who happified
us with their company.

We passed the first week in our new quarters
very contentedly.   Our room was warm and comfortable, large and easy of access, and we wondered
how our handlord could afford to bestow upon us so
much accommodation for so little money, as our
board only amounted to twelve dollars a week, while
several single persons belonging to our troupe
were paying quite that amount.

Business at the theater was excellent.   The Legislature had met, organized and was engaged in the
duties pertaining to legislation.   The city was full
of strangers, each seeking the accomplishment of his
own object; some simply to visit the place for pur-

poses of curiosity or observation, others to perfect commercial transactions, some looking for their success in personal interests through coaxing and cajoling of State senators, representatives, friends and coajutors, while many came to invest capital in various kinds of business. Springfield was really a lively place, full of comers and 'goers, and the center of a most substantial trade with a broad circuit of country.

We had remained in the New England House, as the hotel was called where we stopped, only about two weeks, when one day, just after dinner, I walked out with a friend to be absent only for a short time. Upon my return to my lodgings I found my wife occupied in washing some small articles of clothing in a wash-dish which stood upon a stand to my left as I entered the doorway which was on the north side of our room. I had but just stepped in, when my companion, turning about from the duty in which she was engaged, looked at me with a very serious smile and remarked:

"My goodness, Marcenus, don't you believe, I've had the "rappings" during your absence."

"What do you mean, my dear," said I, as I gazed at her in astonishment.

"I mean," she replied, "that while you was out, and as I stood near the wash-stand ringing out the handkerchiefs and little things which are now out drying, I suddenly felt light concussions under my feet upon the floor, and I recognized them at once as "spirit rappings."

"Did they rap much?" said I, somewhat anxiously.

"At first," she answered, "they commenced on their own account, the sounds being very light and gentle under the bottom of my right foot. As they ceased I requested the spirits to rap again, and louder if possible, when equally—I may say—to my surprise and fear several louder noises were produced."

"Oh, Delia," said I, · half-credulous and half-doubtful of her veracity, "I guess you're trying to play a joke on me, ain't you?"

"Laughing at my want of confidence in what she had said, she very quickly replied:

"No, indeed, I am not trifling; they are truly "spirit rappings," for they sound precisely as those did which I heard in Rochester in the presence of the Fox girls."

Noticing that I had a rather facetious smile upon my countenance, and thinking that my belief in what she was saying was a little *shaky*, she very sincerely as well as suggestively continued:

"You may think that I am not in earnest, but I really am. Now to satisfy yourself step up there near the door to the left of the wash-stand and ask the spirits if they will rap for you "

I at once complied with her request, when equally to my mortification and amazement very distinct noises were produced directly under my feet.

"I guess you are in the right, Delia," said I, as I pondered on the singularity of the occurrance, "but what in the world makes the spirits come here to rap, and that just at this particular time?'

"I don't know," remarked my wife, as she gazed

at me with a rather interested though evidently anxious look, "I don't know; but of one thing I am quite certain, I felt unhappy when I first came into this house, and when I was in this room alone the first day I experienced a very unpleasant sensation of hopelessness and dread."

"Well," said I, "wishing to turn her mind from that drooping seriousness and in quietude which she began to manifest, "let us see if we can't induce the spirits to account for their conduct. Perhaps they'll answer our questions, or communicate with us."

"I have been trying to get them to answer my questions for some time," remarked Delia, "but without any definite satisfaction. The rapping is very much confused and it's impossible to tell whether the sounds are designed as replies to questions or not."

Notwithstanding my wife's assurance that there was no likelihood of my receiving any intelligible answers to the inquiries which I might make, I insisted upon conforming to the good christian apostle's advice, wherein he counseled men to "try the spirits," and so I said:

"Will the intelligence which causes the rappings to be made, consider our desires and endeavor to answer our questions by the usual method, one rap signifying *no*, two *doubtful*, and three *yes*."

A single rap was the answer.

I was satisfied at once that the spirit had misunderstood my question, or otherwise was inclined to display a pugnacious inclination of mind—from personal necessity or some other cause—upon being too closely pressed; for the more I insisted upon a direct reply the more emphatic became the *solemn single sound.*

I continued to ask questions for some time when at last almost despairing of meeting with any success in the object which I had in view—that of getting a consistent and sensible reply to a reasonable inquiry—I was impressed to ask:

"Does the spirit wish us to leave the room which we occupy?"

An emphatic three raps were immediately given, and to this inquiry several times repeated, we unfailingly gained the same unmistakable "yes." Indeed, this was the only straightforward answer given to our questionings, and which never failed to be made when the same inquiry was propounded.

For some time I endeavored to converse with our unseen attendants, but failing to elicit anything conclusive or desirable, I said to my wife:

"Let us not be troubled about the spirits. I don't think, they'll do us any particular harm. If you're willing, I'll get out my violin and play'em a tune."

Laughingly she replied: "Perhaps you'de better; it may make them good natured and more consistent."

No sooner had I taken out my instrument and commenced to play thereon, than the rappings began to be more distinctly heard beating time to the music. This continued for a few moments and then ceased.

Feeling that I had done all I could for once to fathom the singular mystery which had so unexpectedly presented itself in our appartment, I said to my companion who was at the time preparing to go to the public hall where she had to meet her evening obligations:

"This is a most strange affair. Let us not mention the fact of the occurrence of this phenomena in our room to any person, at least not until we know more of its characteristics. It might molest our relations with the landlord, Mr. Trowbridge, and his family, and be a source of serious trouble to us in many ways if we should. To morrow I will see what further progress I can make in obtaining answers to questions, and I will also look into the cellar below and endeavor to learn exactly how we're situated."

"I won't say anything about it," remarked Delia, as she placed in my hand a little box, with a request to carry it to the green-room of the theater, whither we were going.

Receiving the box and taking my little girl by the hand, we three together now made our way out of the hotel into the street, and directed our footsteps at once to the building where our performances were given.

My wife had been in the habit of leaving our Jennett, then in her fifth year of age, in the room we were occupying during brief intervals in her absence, but upon this occasion, through prudence as well as timidity, it was thought advisable to take her with us.

Like most people I naturally had a horror of "tampering ghosts," notwithstanding my desire to comprehend the "laws of life," to reach a knowledge of the "immortality of the human soul," and to understand something of that state of existence which my own kindred in spirit had naturally and unavoidably inherited.

Why spirits should commence to make demonstrations in the particular apartment of the hotel which we occupied, and that to our great annoyance, was a subject of most serious consideration; and the advice which we had received from them requesting us to leave the room only made the riddle still more perplexing.

I had a deep and abiding friendship for the dead. I loved to think that I might meet with the deceased relatives of my Father's household in peace and happiness at the close of my earthly life. My heart reached out in expressable fondness for the Brother whom I had lost, for the Sisters who had departed from my association and knowledge in death, and as I reflected upon the mysterious events of the day, while engaged in selling tickets to our patrons on that memorable evening, I resolved as a result of much reflection to quietly and privately investigate the phenomena to my entire satisfaction, should it continue in the room which we occupied.

Alas! how often are we dissappointed. We returned home from the theater at a quarter to twelve o'clock that night and at once retired to rest. We had no sooner put out the light which we had in use, than the spirits commenced their—to us—

untimely operations. Rappings were made in various
places about our apartment, but being of a gentle
nature—although somewhat undesirable at that particular time of night—we bore their intrusive
presence and noise without complaint, and soon
slept as soundly, perhaps, as if our unseen visitors
had made no demonstrations at all.

The idea that the spirits should manifest themselves by "sounds" whenever *they* saw fit, and especially when we didn't want them to—and that
seemed to be their hobby—was a purpose to me
abusive of every righteous principle of wisdom, and
wholly inconsistent with that goodness, kindness,
generosity or friendly feeling, which men exercise
and display toward one another.

When I asked the spirits to desist from rapping
in the darkness, they very pugnaciously replied by
louder and more numerous noises. The doctrine of evil
spirits, in the absolute, was to my mind very repugnant.
That men were crafty, cunning, malicious and designing, I well knew; but that spirits were inherently
more so, or that they were malignantly inclined at
any time, or in any particular, was to me a thought
as insecure and objectionable as it was unhappy.
Then again another inquiry arose in my mind; it
was this: "Would my good Angel Brother and
Sisters, or the better class of spirits—supposing distinctions to exist among them—permit a dastardly
and impertinent abuse of every just rule of quiet and
loving relationship and communion, when the plain,
honest, sincere purposes of unalloyed friendship and
truth are ever more commended and much more
acceptable?"

I was aware that many tribes and nations in
different portions of the earth were low, degraded
and viciously inclined, but I had no idea that they
could or would come to us after death and molest
our sacred personal rights. For I thought, that
if the principle or doctrine of "angel ministration"
was correct or even needful, then the family circle
upon earth must necessarily be defended against in-
trusion, as well in a heathen land as in a christian
country, by the near relatives of the deceased. I
could not think it wise in the works of the Divine
Author as displayed in the economy of nature to so
condition man in his rudamental existence, as to
make him the subject of torment and distress from
a world or sphere inhabited by unseen beings. Other
reasons were surely to be assigned as the cause
of spirit insincerity, captiousness and cupidity.

It was evident that the spirits could answer
questions correctly if they felt inclined to do so, as
they did in this instance without a single failure
whenever I inquired if we should leave our lodgings.

But wherefore should they insist upon our vacat-
ing a room which we paid for weekly, and which
was in every way cozy and comfortable. There was
a mischief somewhere. We concluded to patiently
wait and learn further concerning the matter through
quiet and private examination and consideration
of the whole subject.

During the second day the sounds occurred but
only at our request. We examined the room, but
found no cause for the raps. I looked into the cellar, and found the noises could not proceed from

that quarter, as there was all of ten inches of water over its entire bottom, and it furthermore was wholly unoccupied as a place of storage or for household purposes.

The second night, as soon as we had retired to rest—the light being extinguished—the spirits begun their noisy jubulation, this time greatly more to our discomfort than previously. I requested them to desist from keeping us awake in the night time, remarking that it was our misfortune to be kept up quite late in the evening in the pursuit of our business, and that we needed the few hours repose which we could secure between midnight and morning.

The spirits disregarding our desires as well as requests, played *merry hob* about the room by hammering first upon this thing and then upon that, until finally a sound like a pistol shot startled my nerves, when I arose from my bed, lit a light, and became as turbulent as a hornet, because the invisible scamps, as I called them, would'nt stop their intolerable meddlesomeness and mischief.

I supposed from the conduct of the spirits that they only laughed at my indignation and worryment of mind, for while their malevolence—if it may be so called—was somewhat abated in the presence of a light, and when I was up and about the room, it was as determinately resumed when I returned to my bed and the light was put out.

I now began to see that the spirits were in real earnest, for I had no sooner returned to my couch than a noise like striking with a raw-hide or more solid leather whip was repeatedly made on the foot board of our bedstead and in other portions of the room. Rappings and a variety of noises, such as scuffling, a sound like a prolonged hiss or whiz, and scraping upon the floor and furniture were repeatedly heard. I again arose from my bed, lit the lamp, which we used and determined to leave it burning during the balance of the night.

I found it difficult to sleep. I was more than usually disturbed. I was fully satisfied that the "invisibles" did not intend to comply with our desires, and that for some reason, more than ordinary, they wished us to leave the room. When the morning came and the manifestations ceased, I said to my companion who was much more annoyed than myself at the unreasonable extent to which the spirits had carried their *frasque*.

"I guess, Delia, I'll quietly ask the landlord for another room. It's not a very happy privilege to remain in an apartment haunted by knowing and truculent ghosts, and rather than do so, I would willingly accept a less comfortable place."

"Yes," said she, "I think we'd better change our quarters. But perhaps they won't allow us to remain in the house."

"O, I guess they will," I replied, "I don't think, they claim to control the entire hotel. They have some special liking to this particular room, and I guess, we'll be more contented when we have given them full possession."

Delia smiled, and as she did so, I observed that she seemed to be deeply engaged in thinking. All at once collecting her thoughts, she looked at me and remarked:

"When the irish chamber-girl came into our apartment yesterday—you being absent—to perform her usual labor, I inquired of her if she knew anything about the handlord's family, when she somewhat hastily answered:

"Indade, I do, and the mischief is in it sure."

"Well," said I, "we've heard some very strange noises in our room since we came here."

"Yes, ma'am, the divel is all about the house. The ould muther is as crazed as a bat, and the landlathy of the house is'nt much bether."

My wife was so delighted with the irish girl's facetious manner of expressing herself, that she went into a hearty laugh as she related what she had said.

I, of course, could not help joining in her mirthful happiness, and so we laughed together, until our "weight of woe" became lightened by temporarily forgetting a sister's troubles, and our own misfortunes and displeasures.

After breakfast was over on the morning to which I have referred, and after the spirits had kept myself and companion awake during an entire night, by thumping and banging about our apartment, I went to the landlord, and without much heart in my enterprise, remarked to him that I wished a room up stairs; that the one which we occupied was dark and dismal and not well suited to please us.

I noticed a very suggestive look, expressed through the eyes and in the countenance of Mr. Trowbridge, as I introduced the subject of the unpleasantness of our apartment. It was evident from his peculiar silence as well as his actions that he was .not without a knowlege of the existence of the phenomena which had annoyed us, but which I had concluded not to mention, unless compelled to by circumstances.

We were immediately shown to a long, narrow room, on the second floor of the hotel, and during the remaining time that we boarded at the New England House we were never troubled by the spirits.

CHAPTER XII.

DR. BELL'S STATEMENT, WITH THOUGHTS CONCERNING THE SPRINGFIELD DEMON-STRATIONS.

While living in the City of Springfield, and subsequently to the occurrence of the events which I have thus briefly related, I made the acquaintance of a gentleman residing in that place by the name of Dr. Bell, whom we afterwards received as our family physician, and with whom I soon became somewhat familiar as a friend and medical adviser.

Upon one occasion he called at the hotel where we were stopping, to make us a visit. While engaged in conversation at that time, I inadvertantly referred to the trouble which we had had with the spirits in the room at first occupied by myself and family in the house. After listening to my recital of the principal facts in the case he said:

"Perhaps I can tell you something that will aid you in accounting for the singular demonstrations of which you speak.'

"Well," said I, "any information which will enable me to reach a knowledge of that mystery will be very acceptable."

After a moment's reflection he began by saying:

"Some time during the early part of last winter, Mr. Wade, the proprietor—at that time—of the New England House, and father-in-law of Mr. Trowbridge, who is now your landlord, had the misfortune to push or throw his son, a young man, then some sixteen or seventeen years old, out of the back door of the hotel. It being very slippery at the time, he fell upon his head and fractured his skull. He was brought into the house, and during the time which intervened previous to his death—which occurred soon after—he occupied the identical room wherein you and your family were at first situated. I attended the young man during his sickness which lasted some time, and done all I could to alleviate his sufferings. During the period of his illness he manifested con-

stant symptoms of mental derangement, and these
increased toward the last,—probably as a result
of accompanying fever—until he became the subject
of raving madness.   He swore and cursed and tore
his hair, and was truly a woeful object of willful
anger and wicked utterance.   He died while heaping
epithets and curses upon everything and everybody
about him."

"Well," said I, "Doctor, that was indeed a very
unhappy circumstance.   I am really thankful for
your statement of facts in regard to, the matter.
The manifestations which the spirits *improvised* in
that room while we remained in it, were truly both
willful and wonderful.   My wife said that she was
unhappy from the moment she entered the hotel,
and even after we had changed our apartment, and
the spirits no longer molested our peace, the same
unpleasant feeling continued for some time to linger
over our joy and composure.   Owing to the circumstance however that we were connected with the
theater here, or thinking that the kindly feeling
of the public toward her as a *danseuse* and actress
might be injured were these things to become known,
we have thus far thought it prudent to make no
mention of the matter, not even to the landlord, his
family, or those connected with our own company."

The doctor smiled as he remarked my discretion,
and said :

"I guess you won't be troubled any more by the
ghosts."

"I hope not," I replied, "the pleasure to be derived from their company, especially when "turbulent,"

is not equal to the misery which they are sure to inflict. For once in my life, Doctor, I must confess, I have found the spirits "in their devices" very unceremonious, if not deeply committed to the pursuit of "wicked ways." They drove us out of our comfortable quarters, don't you believe, and I think it was a most heartless piece of business, so much so that I've given up all hope of ever correcting their "dubious moral characteristics."

The doctor laughed outright at my facetious way of expressing myself on the subject of the abuse which we had received from the invisible occupants of our snug little chamber below, but when his mirthful feelings had somewhat subsided, he very wisely remarked:

"Spirits, allowing that they exist, may not always choose life in wisdom."

At this point in our conversation some one rapped at our door, and the half hours agreeable chit-chat which we had enjoyed together was ended.

The reader will undoubtedly observe from the account which I have herein given of my experience with the spirits in the New England House that I was not pleased with their demonstrations or conduct. They manifested an uncomely principle of intelligence. In fact, every peculiarity exhibited in their deportment was strangely unreasonable and mischievously annoying. The room was what most persons would denominate a "haunted chamber." To me it was a place of unrest. I had no fear of ghosts, hobgoblins or spooks, but I had no desire to quarrel with the dead, and I was well aware that they had

G

every advantage of me by being unseen. Hence I concluded to retreat from the field of conflict and give the spirits their satisfaction in victory.

But laying all jokes aside, and putting every feeling of malice beneath our feet, there are still several important problems which demand our consideration as a consequence of the development of this marvelous phenomena and its singular characteristics. We are not prepared to say *who* it was that caused the strange noises which induced us to leave our room, but we are prepared to say that they were produced as a result of known conditions, and were under the direction of "intelligent mind;" for questions were not only answered, but a discretion, deep and self-chosen was evinced in every reply. The whole transaction afforded irrefutable evidence of the existence of invisible beings, who were possessed of personal thought, power to act, motives held in abeyance of reflection and purposes which were carried into practical effect through the illuminating power of reason.

Whether it was the boy who died so unhappily through intoxication and anger, having inherited as well a malicious disposition to begin with, was a question which to me was not to be hastily decided, yet one concerning which I presumed any person might properly entertain an opinion of their own. In my judgment it was manifest that if the young man died in a state of mental derangement and misery, his freedom from disease through relief in death must very soon enable his mind to return to the exercise of calmness and consideration, as in the ordinary condition of outward life.

This circumstance taken in connection with the
fact of the individual guardianship of spirits, I concluded, must tend to convince the thoughtful that
either no hostile purpose was intended, or else as a
family or personal provision the principle of spirit
ministration was surely involved in doubts and uncertainties, if not implicated in unrighteousness.

It was quite evident from the unwelcome phase
which the demonstrations had assumed in this instance, that the spirit was either displeased and inclined to retaliate for having had to suffer a premature death through a most unhappy combination
of circumstances, or else on the other hand inate
maliciousness of mind was the prompting cause of the
persistent raps and noises which were made in dis-
obedience of my kindly request to the contrary.

It was manifest that familiarity in mental commerce was not desired by the "invisibles," and it was
quite as demonstrable that they were evil-possessed
in the absoluteness of their determination and the
pursuit of the ill-chosen object which they held in
view. I was satisfied from what had occurred in
our room that the passions of the soul, still continued
to hold their jubilee of malice beyond the grave, or
else the conclusion could not be avoided that deliberately calculated mischief was a thing justified in
super-terrestrial circles of life and society.

It had ever been my joy to think well of spirits,
and it was with a feeling of mental oppression that
I regarded this remarkable occurrence. I wanted to
believe that the dead were good, wise, just, considerate and kind. That my own near relatives in

immortality were not only happy, but that they were well disposed and still retained a heart in com- mon with our better desires and knowledge. But my thoughts were shaken. I contemplated the subject of spirit life with more concern, with more serious apprehension than ever before. The rule which I had adopted to think spirits "not evil," not mis- chievous, nor inclined to be intrusive, was broken. I could no longer accept the idea of personal perfection as based upon or as resulting from physical dissolution. Spirits I conceded might justify their conceits and foibles as needful in self-interest, but as mortals we are only supposed to judge "from what we know," and the same in matters of morality and righteousness, as in those of immortality, injustice or wickedness. It is. not within the power or province of the human mind to comprehend the laws or mo- tives by which spirits are governed; but it is within the measure of our wisdom to refuse to accept or pa- tronize a condition of things which to us appears need- less, ignominious or justifiable only in a state of exi- stence of which we have no definite understanding.

It was not my pleasure to think that for any reason, the dead would return to speak with mor- tals—or if not to speak, to silently *mystify* a commerce of thought or phenomena, as between themselves and us—by hampering rules destructive of all satisfaction, if not of that felicity which all mankind seek to enjoy in reaching forward to an understanding of the "future life," and the condition of those whom we have loved, and who have found their reward therein.

As I have hereinbefore hinted, several very important questions arose in my mind as a result of the phenomena which took place in our apartment in the New England House. The idea of physical contact being necessary to the production of the noises was clearly refuted. A mediumship did not exist. The manifestations came wholly unsolicited, and were indeed a part of the free performance accorded to the various occupants of that particular room.

Then again as to how the spirits could cause such a diversity of *sonorous* sounds, their very production implying a knowledge of laws wholly unknown to the wisest earthly minds, was a matter of serious thought. And yet this was not all, for the inquiry, "where were the spirits," was a more perplexing problem and one which I earnestly labored to comprehend.

I did not think it possible for them to be in the room, and still it was quite as difficult for me to believe that they were far from the locality where they were operating. I was quite certain that they must have a fixed situation or position somewhere, and it was equally as evident that for them to be able to exercise such wondrous power, required not only reflection, memory and calculation, but implied the necessity of some form of mental if not of material organization.

As to the manner, in which the raps and noises were produced I was also wholly at a loss to discern. I was aware that the laws termed *accoustic* were involved in the development and propagation of all

sound, and that the atmosphere was its principal
medium. But how sounds could be caused, or the
atmosphere vibrated without the occilating effect
of some *sonorous* body, was a question quite as perplexing as it was unsafe to answer.

The captiousness of the spirits was also a subject of serious reflection. "If it is not within the
limit of desire for the "invisibles" to return in a
peaceful way," thought I, "and it is their purpose to
annoy and torment families and individuals by insincere and fickle methods of manifestation, wherefore
should we be serious, considerate, kind and loving
toward them."

My brother had been dead at the time of the
occurrence of the Springfield demonstrations herein
narrated just ten years, and I concluded—believing
him to be my Guardian Watcher—that he was
either unable to prevent the newly arisen spirit
of Young Wade,* from pursuing a mischievous purpose in his ultra-mundane life, which purpose was
provoked as a result of very unfortunate conditions
and circumstances upon earth, that he was not
willing to interpose his *will* in behalf of the peace
of myself and family, that he *could not control* my
spiritual interests—I being the ward of his protecting
care—in the society and household where I was
living, or on the other hand his life was not what I
had been led to desire, and I could do nothing less
than hold him accountable for being implicated in
an unpleasant if not reprehensible transaction.

Thus I reasoned concerning this singular phenomena, and although my individual views are to
day, some sixteen years after its occurrence, greatly
changed, the convictions which I then formed were
not impertinent to the facts established, neither so
easy of disproval as many worthy thinkers might
suppose; for notwithstanding absolute knowledge
was in this, as it is in many other cases, seemingly
unattainable, still it must be conceded that the
evidence disclosed tended to substantiate opinions
identical with those to which I have herein given
expression, and moreover it is universally acknowledged that the analogical and synthetical processes
of thought and consideration—the only means to be
employed in the attainment of knowledge in a case
like this—are not only reliable as a basis for the
support of ultimate opinions, but equally so far the
founding of a final judgment upon any subject
whatsoever.

CHAPTER XIII.

POPULAR PREJUDICES. MISS IRISH, THE MEDIUM.

Some time toward the close of the month of February, in the year 1859, Mr. Charles Fisher, a personal friend of my Father's family, and who lived in Victor, Ontario County, New York, where we then likewise resided, came to our house in the absence of myself and wife, being accompanied by a "rapping medium" whose acquaintance he had formed in the City of Rochester, where she had been engaged in giving public *seances* in private families.

The medium's name was Miss Sarah J. Irish. She was a person whose features and personal appearance were somewhat unhappily attuned to the objects of hasty familiarity or friendship, yet the prominent characteristic of her life which was a mediumship for "physical manifestations," more than usually wondrous, tended in a measure to qualify her less flattering peculiarities, and cause her to be accepted where otherwise she would not have been cordially received.

Mr. Fisher had called at our residence to secure accommodation for the Medium, who was engaged in giving public "sittings" and exhibitions of "spirit rapping" as a means of gaining a livelihood, and of convincing investigators of the truth of the immortality of the human soul, and the possibility of spiritual intercourse—knowing also that I was soon to return home, and that I still had a desire to more thoroughly examine the subject of spiritualism in its physical aspects and phases. Indeed, Brother Fisher and myself were mutually interested in seeking for a knowlege of the cause and value of the "mysterious manifestations," and of better deciding the question of the righteousness of our fealty to the doctrines and teachings of the "New Philosophy," which was then being freely discussed by many wise and worthy thinker both in Europe and America.

Mr. Fisher had released himself from the domineering influence of early sectarian schooling, and was sincerely devoted to a belief in the general principles of spiritualism; but as in my own experience he had met with an insincere and studied opposition to the views which he entertained and sought to advance, and as this obstinacy of the public mind arose from causes over which no mortal could wield the least control, it was apparent to him as well as to myself that to be self-just, required either personal silence or the exercise of ample circumspection in the promulgation or advocacy of ideas and opinions upon a subject at once so new and irresponsible.

Spiritualism was as yet extremely unpopular, and to seek its gospel openly, was by many still regarded as a criminal offense against the staid "tenets of faith" which slumbered so watchfully in the upholstered christian synagogues of the land. Jeers and sneers were often heaped upon our devoted desires and belief, and unfeeling epithets were freely used by those who claimed to represent in practice the doctrines of Love and Forbearance.

It required courage to meet the pugnacious and dominating ideas of the then existing, shy and crafty opposition. I was more taciturn of mind, yet not less determined in the purposes of my knowledge concerning spiritualism, than my friend and brother Mr. Fisher. We had with others plowed the first furrows in the new field of "immortal enterprise," and we smiled when the old fogies in religious assumption said that they would *laugh us out of our opinions.*" Sometimes they got caught in the mire of their own mistakes by a slippery argument, then again we got a rebuff by a period from the pen of some owlish monk, secreted behind his latinized Euphonisms and sententious remarks.

Spirit manifestations we were fearless to investigate. Not everything did we accept; but using our best discretion, we received those facts and arguments which were self-supporting and undeniable, never forbidding ourselves the righteous privilege of seeking for information, even though at the cost of a "prevailing sense of propriety."

We pursued our purpose under the instigation of a belief in *self-consent.* Knowing that men connived at justice, lauded mothered godlessness in high places, and fingered the dirt of wealth to shy the logic of mental aprisal, we thought that a search for the "treasures of knowledge," when supported by manliness and true honor, should be permitted in friendship, and commended as personally unharmful.

But community said "no." The deacons of our christian fatherhood must consider and settle all important questions. The "Devil" is the "guard of unrighteousness," and must be looked after. He is the "despoiler," and spiritualism with many other new-fangled notions are "of his consent."

Thus we bore the burthen of our own opinions, studied our own proprieties, and while we sought to impose our convictions upon no person, we, at the same time, availed ourselves of many opportunities to disseminate the views which we entertained and cherished. It was not so much our regard for our personal sentiments, or special devotion to the "spiritual philosophy," that provoked a determination on our part to advance our own ideas and sentiments, as it was our purpose to maintain the admirable principle of the "right of private judgment," a doctrine taught by every wise and unselfish protestant christian since the days of the Lutherean reformation.

Spiritualism was to us not a *perfect* system of philosophy, but a *promising* school of ethics, well calculated to elevate our thoughts, enhance the value and increase the amount of our knowledge. It recognized the "law of progress," and supported the utmost "freedom of thought." No hampering rules or arbitrary conditions were imposed upon those who sought consolation from its teachings. It was a source of joy to the heart, of satisfaction to the understanding, and was "nature's own religion." It taught us that we were immortal; that mind lived in the enjoyment of self-conscious life forever; that the translated soul was still. *itself* in all things which pertained to individuality in existence.

From the investigation of spiritualism we obtained direct and irrefutable evidence of the immortality of the soul. It was no guess-work. The departed returned to speak with mortals by their own permission. The methods adopted by the spirits in their communion with us were not, perhaps, always suited to our pleasure, but the *fact*, the *certainty* of spiritual intercourse was by these processes clearly demonstrated. The *ifs* and the *ands* were omitted. Our relatives and the countless hosts of earth's departed children were by the modes employed clearly revealed to our recognition, although in *mystery*.

Proprietitious church members adviced us to let spiritualism alone. Our circumstances rendered it necessary that we should in part hoodwink our own opinions. But like the author of the idea of the earth's rotary motion, we presumed to be stubborn in our well-founded views, and howbeit the gag-i-lasting objections of old fogies, and men of settled and unalterable convictions, we did occasionally give utterance to the expressions "the world moves," "spiritualism is true," or something to that effect.

We were invited by the churches to relinquish our faith. The Presbytereans, straight-jacketed in

all things, sought to direct us in the "narrow path,"
which those of "their lessons" were said to follow in
their journey to the "kingdom of heaven." The
Methodists commending themselves as the "chosen
authority" in "scriptural interpretation," and falling
into jubulations of psychology under the name
of "religious revivals," sought our "salvation," advising
us that there was uncertainty in regard to our
safety in the future, if we did not "repent of our
sins." The Universalists usually accounted a "liberal
religious sect," in their "holy mission of love" sought
to protect us in our worship, but through inadvert-
ancy, priestcraft or bewilderment of mind, they
suddenly forgot a worthy precept in the catalogue
of "christian virtues," and refusing us even the
hope, the consolation which we derived from the
use of the humble basement of their "crumbling
edifice," gave us the "highly exampled" privilege
of outdoor worship.

Between these and other contending religious
forces and factions, which were also mutually
watchful of each other's cares and interests, especially when what they considered "foreign aggression"
seemed eminent, we found our spiritual "faith" a
burthensome object of personal solicitude. But notwithstanding the interposing obstacles and the
ill-adviced opposition which the churchiological
sadducees of modern manacled thought saw fit to
manifest toward us, we cheerfully hummed the merry
song of "joy be with thee," nor heeded the outcry
of "humbug" the ever unmeaning epithet, to frequently employed in derision of subjects the most
worthy and truths the most startling and grand.

In the absence of myself and companion the medium had remained at my Father's house, which was also our home, some seven or eight days. Upon our return, however, we found that she had gone to the City of Syracuse, but with a distinct understanding that she would remain absent only for a short time.

"Who is Miss Irish," said I to my Mother, who had been engaged in conversation with my wife concerning the medium and the rappings soon after our arrival, "who is she; where did she come from, or what are her personal antecedents?"

"Well," she replied, "according to her own story she originally came from the South, has lived in Virginia, and more recently in this State. Her parents are not living. She has for some years gained a livelihood by giving exhibitions of spirit rapping in New York, Washington and other cities. A few weeks ago she came to Syracuse, and thence to Rochester. While stopping at Mr. Isaac Post's in the latter city, Mr. Fisher happened to make her acquaintance, and thus invited her to his house."

"What is the appearance of the woman?" said I, continuing my inquiries, "what sort of a person is she? How does she look?"

My mother smiled as she remarked:

"She's a person of fair and slender form, but of *awful* homely features. She is of dark complexion, possessing large, staring and repulsive black eyes, is somewhat awkward in her manners, and on the whole not a person of attractive look or demeanor. While she seemed very kind and pleasant, there was at the same time something about her which was extremely forbidding, and on the whole I am not prepossessed in her favor."

"Well," said I, "she's a good medium, is she?"

"Indeed, she is," was the firm answer, "she gives entire satisfaction. The rappings are loud and distinct in her presence, and she writes communications with great rapidity. These she obtains by repeating the "printer's alphabet," the letters composing the words employed being each indicated by a distinct rap."

My Mother's only complaint seemed to be that the medium was ill-looking, and somewhat inclined to equivocate *ad defensio personum* in conversation, which to her was not altogether a commendable characteristic.

"We are always in more or less doubt," she remarked, "about the worthiness of a person with whom we are not intimately acquainted, and it often requires some time to reach or fathom the peculiarities of those with whom we are not familiar."

"Yes," said I, "but human imperfection is, in my judgment, one of the Divine purposes of creation, and the faults and mistakes of life, like homely forms or distorted features, are not so much deserving of rebuke as of wise and charitable consideration."

"A world of woe is *our* world," remarked my Father, "self-selected propriety is nature's own. In matters of righteousness we are all selfish judges. It is only when personal faults have "burned themselves to purity" that the individual knows how to justly appreciate the "*better way.*"

"We would not refuse to confer with a lunatic,"

said I, "if it served our coffers : why should we refuse to learn wisdom, even though its source be intermixed with repugnant opportunities. The gift
of knowledge is usually greatest with those who seek
no fastidious refuge from the defects and follies
which beset humanity. For my part I shall be glad
to have the medium return, that I may hear the
rappings and acquire a deeper insight into the cause
of spiritualism."

"If Miss Irish is a good medium" continued I
after a moment's thought, that's the most we could
desire. The probabilities are that her being at our
house will create a little "mischievous gossip" among
our more talkative neighbors, but so far as that is
concerned we may bear a moiety of abuse with composure, and I am satisfied that to do so is a sure
guarantee for the ultimate correction of individual
impertinence and uncharitableness in community.
If we should suffer a little at the hands of the
public on account of spiritualism, or in seeking the
"good of the future" in "ways not commended,"
perhaps we may receive our reward in the intelligence which we shall gain. For my part I am
greatly disposed to pilot my own canoe, and guage
the fitness of my own conduct in life, and I have
but little faith in the hatched-up every-day ideas
of propriety, which inhere in the hetcheled relationships of society in country towns.

I still have a wish to investigate this most
singular phenomena, a wish to know the extent
of its truth, and whether it is a cause worthy of our
fullest confidence and esteem. If man is immortal,

and the fact can be rendered comprehensible to the human intellect, it is the most wondrous discovery ever given to satisfy the longings of the soul. Spiritualism, it is true, is quite unpopular; but what new idea, development, or manifestation was ever honored in its juvenescent life. Men are prompted by selfish motives. Honor and honesty are abetted. The truth itself is hoodwinked, and righteousness becomes pretentious. Sincerity is wasted in animadversions, bickering deception and overdone measures of policy, while human happiness is a condition chosen in selfishness and measured by wealth.

To me spiritualism is true. I still love those dear ones who have closed their terrestrial pilgrimage, and who promoted in being still live to be blessed in realms of the unseen and the immortal. If it is a fault to love the departed, then that fault is mine. If spirits malign their own goodness or wisdom by an imperfect selection of *media*, then theirs is the punishment, as also the defeat. Spirits may not always be just, considerate or worthy, but being thoughtful ourselves, reasonable, and on our guard as against the encroachments of wrong, even as we would in dealing with men, so may we avoid any unhallowed spirit influence with which we may meet or have to contend.

The laws of life are with us, and we are all subject to their action. The spirit leaves the body quickly. Wherefore is it so changed that we may not know of its life or destiny? All men are greatly alike in their physical natures, in their mental as

well.   The same correspondence must exist in spirit
life.   The Hottentot is not less safely formed in body
and   mind than the "proud Caucasean." Modern
christians are at fault in making *selection* of souls
for heaven, and consignment of other souls to regions
of distress and wretchedness.   If God permits man
to live in comparative happiness upon earth, in
varied complexion, form and feature, in savagism,
barbarism, civilization and freedom, why should he
be less benevolent in the future immortal sphere?
We can award no curse to the productions of the
Supreme Author.   Our social distinctions and local
hatreds, while perhaps natural to our circumstances,
state of progress and intelligence, cannot be justly
said to be inimical to an ultimate and wise purpose
in the Divine economy of creation.

The spirits may not choose a person to do their
work whom I would choose.   They may have discovered that nature does not *forbid* even the "vile
and wretched," much less those who are the subjects
of unstudied mistakes and faults.   Jesus said to the
malefactors who were crucified beside him:

"To-day shalt thou be with me in paradise."

Now, if it be true that heaven forbids not the
wrong-doer, why should we not think it best to
labor for the correction of the defects, follies, and
wickedness by which we are surrounded, rather than
shrug our shoulders and evade all contact there-
with.

The world is full of wretchedness, our cities are
a malstrom of mischief, deceitful motives in trade,
high-handed outrages in financial transactions, and

pillage and theft by the poor, are too common to be made the exception to a principle of honor, and hence must be regarded as a general purpose, unhappily observed as actuating, prompting, and governing hundreds and thousands of persons in every day life.

Twenty thousand homeless females are said to wander by night in the streets of New York city alone, to barter away their comliness of being for the moiety required in life's daily support. Clerks and agents purloin from the means intrusted to their care. Rail-road conductors enrich themselves from perquisites never self-denied. "Red-tape" and "shoddy" are the world's arbitrament. Both the success and happiness of life are too often secured through human abasement, misery and suffering.

In view of these facts, who is to settle the question of individual righteousness? The person of agreeable manners, good looks and pleasant speech may be too deeply gifted in deceit for our discernment. The well dressed falsifier knows his advantage, and through artful maneuvering, comly suavity and palaver, sells the honest, unsuspecting man out to a disadvantage with a *sang froid.*

Experience is always a personal blessing. It confers everlasting benefits. If we are cheated once, the second time we are not to be caught. We become more watchful, more circumspect. It developes our individuality, engenders thought, and substantiates life's rewards. I have not as much fear of personal injury from mediumistic contact, as I have of the inadvertent gossip of many of my friends and neighbors, and the *unfeeling* solicitude which they too often manifest for my individual welfare. I have seen several years of travel, have met and studied the peculiarities of men and women in various positions in society, and I must say, that if nature transmits *its own*, it would not be surprising if we should discover a little cupidity or maleficience in life among the residents of the aereal world, as well as upon earth."

Thus we freely conversed together in our family circle at home concerning spiritualism, the rappings and public sentiment, as it was likely to develope itself, should Miss Irish return and continue her *seances* at our house.

So far as I was personally concerned, I was determined to avail myself of every opportunity to investigate the phenomena of spiritualism, in order to satisfy my desire in regard to an understanding of its cause, and to reach, if possible, a knowledge of the laws involved in its production, to determine likewise, whether it resulted from the action of spirits, or was a manifestation of some hitherto unknown law of life.

I felt no inclination to treat the subject with derision. It was too serious a matter. I had considered my immortal interests for more than twenty years, yet had never fully substantiated the belief which I entertained. Positive knowledge was needed and that I resolved to seek for and find.

CHAPTER XIV.

CONVICTIONS. PRIVATE SEANCES AND FRIENDLY MESSAGES FROM THE UNSEEN.

On Thursday, the twenty-eighth day of February, in the year 1859, while I was absent from home during a part of the day, the Medium, Miss Irish, returned from her journey to the City of Syracuse, and when I arrived soon after, I found her seated in our sitting room and engaged in a pleasant conversation with my wife and mother.

Stepping into the apartment where they were, I was at once introduced and soon became a participant in the social chit-chat which was going on.

I had concluded to search the "deep profound" pertaining to the lady's characteristics. I rambled in reflection to find subjects of worthy interest to converse about. I sought to fathom her individual peculiarities as a beginning in the investigation of her claims to spiritual mediumship. I studied her motives, considered her actions, weighed her words, measured her thoughts, and contemplated the value of every feature represented in her daily life.

That the woman was inadvertently mischievous was apparent. That she was *awful homely*, as my mother said, was a truth which no one could possibly deny. That she was a person of good heart, generous, kind, and confiding, with a strong disposition to cooly avenge real or fancied personal injuries, was also manifest. She was of very dark complexion, a brunette, with black eyes as wondrous in their size and appearance, as they were evidently the source of her greatest mental ability.

After conversing with her for an hour or more, I concluded that like all mortals she lived in imperfection, and supported her own defects. She had lived in Louisiana in her childhood, had subsequently found a home in Virginia, was left without parents, and ultimately cast upon her own resources to secure a livelihood. At all events such was the story which she gave concerning herself.

In her thirteenth year of age she began to hear the rappings, and they had continued to accompany her from that day onward. She was advised by the spirits, followed their counsel, and accepted the mission which they saw fit to confer. At her solicitation her unseen guardian was ever ready to communicate. She had learned to read the printer's alphabet, and repeating it with great rapidity, could in a few mintes cover a sheet of foolscap with letters indicated by the sounds. During the evening of the day of her arrival. our family, together with several other persons, united in a circle about a large table in our sitting room to listen to the noises and receive such messages and answers to questions as the "invisibles" might see fit to impart.

I at once observed that the raps produced in the presence of Miss Irish were identical in sound with those which I had heard in the Fox Family, and later in the room occupied by myself and wife in the New England House during our sojourn in Springfield, Illinois, but a winter or two previous. They were more systematically given however, and served a purpose almost telegraphically perfect as a means of intercourse with the spirit intelligences who claimed to be the cause of their production.

Nothing could be more orderly. They rapped on the table and on the floor. Loud and distinct concussions representing a person walking up stairs, the footsteps gradually dying away, were repeatedly produced. Sounds as of a man sawing off a board with a hand-saw, and others like the noise of a plane at a carpenter's bench were also heard. Many *mental questions* were asked and answered, all to the pleasure and satisfaction of the questioners. A message was given to a gentleman who formed one of the circle and who was a stranger to all present, which purported to come from his father whose name together with that of three other deceased members of his family were mentioned therein. Upon inquiry it was found that the names were all correctly given, that every question had been truthfully answered. The evidence was overwhelming. The gentleman there and then acknowledged his belief in the genuineness of the phenomena which he had wit-

nessed, and has from that time—now better than
thirteen years—remained a spiritualist.

During the sitting, which lasted about one hour,
I interrogated the spirits both by oral and mental
methods, in order to test their ability, as well as
their willingness to concede to human desire in the
matter of social intercourse, and for the purpose
of studying into and reaching, if possible, a knowledge of the means employed, and of the motives
which were engaged in prompting the "immortals"
to produce the physical manifestations which we
witnessed.

In the course of the evening the spirits called
for the alphabet to be repeated for my benefit,
when the following brief communication purporting
to be given by my oldest sister, then some twenty-
two years deceased, was quickly received:

"Marcenus, I wish you to know, that we, your
spirit friends, *are ever near you, and enjoying ourselves
in your society*, although by you unseen. Your
Brother Jacob is most anxious to converse with you.
I often try to influence Father to write. His spirit
is coming nearer and nearer to us, as a result of
mental attraction and the decay of the earth-casket.
When his mortal career is closed, we—a band of us—
will be near to welcome his spirit home to our
sphere.

I am, dear Brother M., your ever-loving sister
Caroline, now of the spirit life. I shall often visit
you."

After some general conversation in which all
the members of our little gathering more or less

indulged, the alphabet was again called for by the spirits, when I at once asked the question:

"Who is it that wishes to communicate?"

To which the spirit at once replied:

"It is your Brother Jacob and Sister Jennett."

The sounds were now continued in telegraphic order, and the following message was given:

"I have studied philosophy *here*, and have learned much concerning the Divine law which governs the movements of matter in its varied forms. The cause of motion in matter, and the law of assimulation as represented in the growth of all organic forms, are well understood by us. I would like to tell you something concerning what we observe in nature—looking as we do through its very folds—and I would do so were it not that this method of communion is so exceedingly tedious, and it would be agreeable to you, I too would tell you of our *sunsets*, of our *valleys and plains*, of our *crystal streams*, of our *pavillions*, of our manner of *constructing them*, of our mode of travel, and last of all of our diving into the earth's atmosphere to visit our friends. Of these many subjects which would you choose? I will speak to you of either as best I can when opportunity offers. I am still Jacob, your loving Brother, but my form is now much smaller than it was when I was with you, and I am more than twenty-one."*

The reader will observe in these communications something to admire and something to consider. It

* He died at that age.

H

is a misfortune to spiritualism that the many
messages received from the other life are not more
thoroughly criticised. It is a mistake of the *heart*
that we do not sift every word and line transmitted
to us from the spirit world for the meanings
which they contain. We love our departed friends
with too much confidence. Our devotion to them
causes us to neglect a proper analysis of their
impartations. When men and women become wise,
discreet, discerning and free from hasty desire,
impulsive ambition, and selfish motives, then the
mind, the only arbiter of destiny, will yield a
reward justly founded in reason and ever safely to
be accepted.

I read these little messages from the higher
life over and over again. It was a concession which
I had not expected. They contained happy thoughts,
were suggestive of others, and yet withall I saw not
the source from whence they came. I had the confidence to believe that it was my Sister and Brother
who had thus spoken with me. But where were
they? How far away? At what *point* or *place*?
These were the thoughts which sought an asylum in
the province of my more serious reflections.

Spiritualists, I knew, differed upon this subject,
some asserting that the soul mounted the heavens
and lived amid the elements of space; others that
the mind in its immortal condition wandered among
the stars, following its own inclinations and delights,
and going and returning at its pleasure. Then again
others, basing their conclusions upon their own ideas,
infered that spirits lived near them, passing out and

in their dwellings, through closed doors, brick walls and all impedements. The christians not less than the spiritualists had their own peculiar notions. Some supposing that the soul, immediately after death, found a residence with God, a very indefinite and intangible thesis. Others held to the opinion that the good alone were "taken home to Christ," which is another undefined proposition, while still another class found an equally mysterious *place of misery* for a large portion of the human race.

The communications which I had received only tended to prompt a desire in my mind to grasp, if possible, a more definite, reliable and comprehensive idea concerning the whereabouts of my spirit friends. I wished to know where they lived, how they lived, and why they lived. The love which I had bourne my Spirit-Brother for so many years, was kindled into a heart-felt affection by the kindly message which had been imparted to my keeping, but certain portions thereof were inscrutable to my perception, were dark and unfathomable.* I was lost to know the *how*, the *why* and the *wherefore.* I could not believe without understanding. I desired to *know*, whatever might be the truth in the premises, for, thought I, in knowledge only is there satisfaction.

We continued to hold circles at our residence for something like three weeks, during which time many strangers came in to satisfy their curiosity, love of the marvelous, or for purposes more sincere and worthy. The spirits were always prompt in replying

*The reader will find the portions here referred to set in Italics.

to inquiries, in transmitting messages, and complying with the demands of investigators. They never failed. The gift of mediumship was most perfect.

I made myself acquainted with the methods adopted by the spirits in answering questions, in giving communications, in producing the sounds. I soon learned to catch the letters from the lips of the medium as she repeated the printer's alphabet. This was at first quite difficult, owing to the rapidity with which the letters were designated. But I soon reached a proficiency in this art which was to me quite surprising.

One evening my Father, who had become somewhat interested in the rappings, seated himself near the medium while we were holding a *seance* when his elder Brother—in answer to his request—who had died in his youth, signified his desire or willingness to communicate. The alphabet was at once repeated and the following message given :

"What shall I say, Brother Thomas? I have been so long in spirit life that I feel but little attraction toward things of mortal consequence. I cannot tell you much concerning our condition. Be assured that my affection has survived our long separation of near half a century, and that I often molest my joy by a peaceful observation of your cares. I still have the same mechanical tastes which gave me so much happiness upon earth, and I find that all the knowledge which I gained while there —*no matter of what kind or nature*—proves to my advantage here. I cannot say more.

Your brother, JOHN WRIGHT."

CHAPTER XV.

CONSCIENTIOUS SCRUPLES.   TRAVELING WITH THE SPIRITS.   A PRAYER.

Miss Irish had been at our house but a few days when, as we were seated at breakfast one morning, my wife remarked:

"Marcenus, why dont you take Sarah and go to some of the villages near by, and give a few public *seances?* There is sufficient curiosity existing in regard to the subject of the rappings, I should think, to enable you to make it a paying enterprise. We are in need of home comforts and if you could make a few dollars in this way, it would help us."

"Well" said I, "I have no particular objection to so doing, but certain I am, that if I go out with Sarah, I shall get besmeared all over by all sorts of gossip."

"That may be," she answered, "but you mus'nt mind what people say. You can go to a few towns within reasonable distance and see what you can do. You've been in the show business long enough to know how to manage affairs, and I certainly would try. If you will take a horse and buggy and go to Macedon, Walworth and Pultneyville, I have no doubt but that you will find the friends of spiritualism willing to receive you and give you aid in your undertaking."

"Well," said I, "the mischief is in it, but I'm as poor as a church mouse, and I guess I'll go out for a week or two and see if I can make anything by it."

As we sat down in the circle that evening to listen to the rappings and converse together the following cousel was given by the spirits for my benefit:

"You are about to engage in an occupation which will reward you in one sense, but in another it will be your misfortune. We shall be with you and watch over you in your trials. We shall help you through with whatever you undertake, whenever it is possible. We shall advice you by impression when we can, and when we cannot, by some plainer method. At a proper time we will give you such needful instruction as to organizing your circles as may be required."

After reflecting for some days upon my wife's suggestion to make a public exhibition of the Spirit Manifestations as given through the mediumship of Miss Irish, and after having made my arrangements in advance, by letter, for holding *seances* in four different places, I took a carriage and with the Medium went out to cancel the engagements which I had promised to fulfill.

In neither place was I disappointed. The spirits were faithful in every particular, and upon every occasion. In one public audience some twelve messages were given during a single evening, covering nearly a sheet of foolscap each, and each containing from one to three names of the deceased relatives of the persons—strangers—to whom they were given.

This was one of the finest tests of spirit identity which had ever come to my knowledge, and I still look upon it as one of the most remarkable upon record. Better than twenty names of spirits, once mortals, and relatives of persons unknown to the medium, and who were present in the audience, were given within an hour and twenty minutes, and not a single mistake was made.

Day after day I watched with a critical eye the various demonstrations which were given. The spirits were at all times ready and willing to bestow upon us that advice and counsel which was deemed essential to our success, and many times to converse with us for an half hour or more in kindly intimacy. But I noticed that the law of *mystery* was still the arbitrary principle, the controlling motive, deeply inwrought in every design of the "invisibles." When pressed with questions which they did not wish to answer, they would either remain silent, or in literary artfulness reply by well-conceived equivocation. In this I discovered wondrous wisdom, and the more I considered this singular feature of the phenomena, the more surprised I became that those persons who had made themselves the most familiar with spiritualism, had not discovered this ever-uppermost char-

acteristic. With some individuals the spirits were
ever ready to converse; with others tolerably so,
while with the majority they seemed comparatively
indifferent, entering into communion only when urgently solicited. The presence of some persons was
strangely repugnant, and the spirits would suspend
intercourse altogether while they were seated in the
circle.*

On several occasions the spirits rapped upon my
boots, also upon my legs while seated by a table,
and at times upon the open palm of my hand within
eighteen inches of my eyes. The impression thus
made was like the sensation which might be felt by
the precipitation of a soft cotton ball against the
flesh. I conceived it to be simply an enforced or
transmitted ball of condensed ethers of an atmospheric or electric quality, for as these balls of fluid
atoms came in contact with the flesh of my open
hand, I realized their flattening tendency and disorganization.

While at Pultneyville on the shore of Lake
Ontario, in Wayne County, New York, where we
remained some ten days in the family of Mr.
Randolph Reynolds, a man much respected, of generous impulses, and agreeable disposition, and whose
whole-souled companion—now deceased—was a woman of nervous inclinations, yet possessed of the

*It has been supposed by spiritualists that the auric principle emenating
from some persons prevents "harmonious conditions," and that spirits cannot
make the manifestations in their presence. I think the future will disclose that
it is in the knowledge which the immortals possess of us personally that this
refusal to communicate is made. The closest shades of difference in the mental
peculiarities of men are to them clearly discernable. Want of sincerity, honesty,
uprightness, kindness, goodness, sobriety or wisdom is by them quickly perceived.

kindest heart and the most eminent virtues, I was
one day impressed to make a respite of my time,
when leaving the house which was a little cottage
near the village, I wandered away alone across the
fields to a distance of some mile or more, and seating myself upon a little eminence where stood some
half-grown ragged pines, I turned my thoughts upon
the subject of my experience.

I was sad. The more I contemplated the
phenomena of spiritualism the deeper became the
puzzle. I had endeavored to reach bottom in my
effort to solve the problem of spiritual communion.
I had succeeded, only for this—the spirits were the
dictators, and quaintly remarked, "thus far thou
shalt go and no farther."

For five consecutive weeks I had watched every
motive which actuated the medium and governed
the manifestations. I had kept a record of every
conversation which I had held with the spirits,
of every message which I had received—these are
still in the possession of the author with many
communications given to other persons—and by
comparison of fact with fact and circumstance with
circumstance I knew that I had not sought in vain
for a knowledge of the truth of the immortality
of the human soul; but I saw that the captiousness,
the contradictions, the frequent insincerity and
strange peculiarities, the evasive replies made to
inquiries, and at times the refusal to concede to the
requests of individuals, was not, as I had been in a
measure led to infer, a result growing out of the
personal ignorance and wickedness of the departed,

but of deep perception, design and profound knowledge in regard to the needs of the world in matters pertaining to intercourse with higher spheres, or otherwise spirit life was conducive to mental misery and misfortune.

I found that I had gone as far in my investigation of the "spirit rappings" as it was desirable to proceed. The spirits themselves had set a limit to explanations by a *rule in deceit*—happy answers, well-worded, beautifully conceived in thought and always very applicable to the question—and when pursued in argument either remained silent, or ejected a score of pleasing sentences to avoid a direct issue.

The Spirits had been familiar with me, had counseled me; but my interrogatories, when conceived in a feeling of criticism, were artfully evaded. Thus I had gone to the end, and I concluded that greater concessions to human demand were forbidden by some established law governing the dwellers in the realms of the invisible, or otherwise, as a result of the possession of more exalted wisdom, it was deemed impolitic by individual immortals to become more intimate with men.

The medium, although not unmindful of the exercise of some of the better qualities of the human heart, manifested a strange demeanor, and in her appearance was as I infered many times, the objection of comers and goers. Only the marvelous mystery which attended her, as an agent of unseen intelligences, aroused public interest and caused her to be accepted with privilege and consideration.

I had studied her characteristics, had measured her capacity of mind, viewed her thoughts, considered every motive which actuated her in her dealing, and in her various conversations, and while it was not within the province of my desire to change the conditions which were represented in her life and mental status, I constantly experienced an unsought repugnance to her presence, and wondered why the beings of the invisible world chose to employ her in the performance of a mission so uninviting, yet so extraordinary.

As I contemplated the circumstances which surrounded my situation, and thought of my family at home, while looking out upon the broad waters of Lake Ontario, I sighed, my heart beat with rapid throbs and my eyes filled with tears. The cold March wind moaned through the slender branches of the scraggly pines hard by. The fretful waves lashed the gravelly beach, and kept up an incessant roar. As far as the eye could reach, the rolling white-caps seemed to rise, and following each other through foam and surf, soon exhausted themselves in the phantom pursuit.

I walked along the shore and listened to the mournful and monotonous music of the tumbling billows. I looked up into the sky. A nest of fleecy clouds floated over my head. I was sad, disconsolate, and my thoughts being attuned to a mood of prayer I said:

"Oh, Merciful Spirit of Nature, give me that comfort which I so much yearn to possess. Give me

that knowledge, so desirable, which saves the mind
from anxiety, hopelessness and misery.   Wherefore,
Oh Father of goodness, are we tantalized and tor-
mented in life?   The world of humanity suffers.
Unholy devices, crafty motives, unhallowed and
untrustworty purposes are the object of all human
trade and traffic.   Candor, sincerity, honesty, justice
and truth are ignored or hampered in expression, by
the controlling power of wealth and selfish personal
interests.   Spirits possessed of wondrous intelligence,
and more wondrous' influence over humankind, live
above us in the air.   They are strange beings.
They live near us all unseen.   In their communion
with mortals they garble a judgment in wisdom.
They will not concede to human dictation.   They
play fantastic tricks in literature, and *shade* a life
of joy, by what—in our discernment—we can only
denominate unnecessary falsehoods and evasions.   Oh,
Kind Parent of Creation, why this singular admixture of light and darkness, of virtue and degradation,
of justice and injustice, of kindness and cruelty.   Is
nature embroiled in never-ending strife, that man
may inherit folly, imperfection, and wretchedness?

We look to the future with hope.   The heart
beats with imotions of joy and satisfaction when the
mind contemplates its prospects in eternity.   Yet
with all our care for the life which is to come, we
are willing to barter away the "goods of righteousness" for mammon, and the *acccepted* opinion of the
world.

Here, Oh Father of infinite wisdom, in ways unsought and unexpected come from their invisible

abode the spirits of the dead. An angel's life is looked upon by mortals as just and holy, but in their communion with men they often manifest characteristics not worthy of our admiration, respect or confidence.

I have loved, Oh Spirit of Supreme Power, the thought that I might be blessed with happiness in my immortal life; that I might meet my spirit kindred beyond the grave with joy, happiness and a freedom from those imperfections so peculiar to our earthly being. But here is evidence of the continuation of mortal defects and individual -waywardness. Wherefore should spirits falsify, wherefore deceive, wherefore annoy us by mysterious announcements and unhallowed insinuations.

Do thou, Oh Spirit of Eminent Mercy, teach us the lesson of thy purposes, and if our existence is to be forever intermingled with pleasure and pain, with wisdom and ignorance, with righteousness and unrighteousness, with satisfaction and disappointment, with delightful thoughts and sorrowful moods, give us the light of understanding that we may provide ourselves with strength to bear our adversities, while parrying the powers of evil, and endeavoring to avoid the mistakes and misfortunes which cling to destiny."

CHAPTER XVI.

CONTEMPLATIONS.   STRANGE FEELINGS.
A VOICE OF COUNSEL.   SPIRIT MESSAGES.

Dear reader, could you love the spirits as well after they had falsified many times in your presence, as you could, if you knew them to be always frank, open, honest, sincere and thruthful?

Nay, you could not.

I had placed the holiest confidence in the "immortals," but now experience was clothing that confidence with doubts and uncertainties. The spirits were altogether self-determined in every purpose. They seemed to disregard my devotion to the principle of goodness and honor; but when I reasoned with myself, I was equally confounded with the impertinence, dishonesty and untruthfulness of men, and thus I concluded that the spirits came honestly by their faults, or otherwise, if they had outgrown them, and still persisted in following evil ways, it was an evidence of a purpose on their part to forbid us that joy in a knowledge of their condition of being which we so much yearned to possess, or else the change of death was unpromotive of right-eousness.

Perhaps, thought I, I anticipate too much from spirits. It may be to their interest to confound human understanding. Spirit life may be too delightful to be revealed to us; else it may be that the chill of the passions in death renders the intellect rigidly cold and unfeeling. At all events, whatever may be the cause of the confusion which is discoverable in their communion with us, its bickerings cannot be reconciled with our ideas of goodness or propriety.

The spirits had by inuendo committed them-selves to the advocacy of a license *ad conubium infesto* of the affections. To me this was distressing. My eyes began to open. Spirits, said I, are natives of the earth. The God, who made man to suffer physical and mental anxieties and misfortunes, has caused the spirit to represent a propinquity of mind.

I had been sincerely devoted in my attachment to my Spirit Brother. He had died when I was young. I thought of him as an angel guardian in whom I could put my trust and repose my confidence. Was I to be dissappointed? Was my Brother not better as a spirit than as a mortal?

It may be, thought I, as I reflected, that my Brother has no personal control of these manifest-ations. It may be that the medium's guardian represents *himself* in this matter, to suit some selfish caprice of mind.

I now turned my footsteps toward the comly little cottage where we were stopping. I walked along the well-washed beach admiring the waves, as they chased each other onward and died away upon the shore. As I stooped to pick up some beautiful pebbles which lay in my path—my heart still drooping with feelings of sadness—that I might admire their smooth round forms and variagated colors, a sense of dizziness suddenly came upon me, which almost threw me to the ground. I sat down for a moment upon an old log to get relief. My eyes sparkled with a new and singular illumination. All of my senses were affected. I put my hand to my brow hoping thereby to press away my pain; but all to no effect. A more oppressive dizziness came over my being. A halo of light issued from my mind. I began to feel distressed, anxious, and my thoughts were robed in uncertainty. Perhaps five minutes had elapsed, during which time I was struggling to release myself from my peculiar realizations and the influence which seemed to grasp the very centre of my consciousness, when, as if from out of the air above my head, a voice uttered these words:

Be—peaceful—quiet—contented—and—fear—not.

I looked up with surprise, the wind sighed and whistled through the fences and across the fields. It was getting colder, or otherwise my sense of feeling was benumbed. I rose up and stood still for a moment thinking of the words which had come to my ear. The sudden blindness and mysterious whirling of my head ceased in a moment, and I at once felt greatly relieved. My mind soon became

clearer, and a feeling of boyancy and hope began to
infuse my entire personality. Experiencing at last a
sensation of chilliness from too long exposure without, I now hastened onward to the house, where I
found the happy comfort of a warm fire, and being
soon called to tea, partially forgot—in the sociable
chit-chat of the hour—the singular event of the
afternoon.

The evening *seance* given by the medium was
well attended, as it had been previously announced to
be her last in the village. The spirits seemed unusually willing to accomodate all inquirers; answers to
questions were readily given, and truthful communications were written *impromptu*. No mistakes
were made. Every one in the circle seemed perfectly
satisfied, and the setting closed with a general sense
of gladness and good feeling.

The next day being Saturday, I had concluded
to return home. My wife had written me that
letters had been received which needed to be
answered at once. Rising, therefore, somewhat early
in the morning and making the necessary preparation, taking a warm breakfast and bidding adieu to
the kind family of Mr. Reynolds, we stepped into
our carriage and were soon out of sight of the
pleasant little village of Pultneyville. It was spring-
time, and the roads being muddy, we were some
seven hours in driving thirty-two miles, the distance
to my father's dwelling.

Upon my arrival home I found letters asking
for the medium to visit LeRoy, Batavia, Albion and
other places in the western part of the State of New

York, but owing to local demands upon my time
these invitations were all declined with the cxcep-
tion of that from LeRoy, which place we visited at
the solicitation of Mr. S. Chamberlin at whose commodious residence we remained some two weeks
giving public exhibitions of the phenomena of spiritualism.

The presence of my wife who accompanied us
on this occasion, and who occupied a seat in our
circles, seemed to greatly increase the strength of
the manifestations, and add a genial influence to the
objects which we had in view. Our circles were
thronged. Many of the best people in the place
were induced to visit the spirits. Lawyers, clergy-
men and doctors came in to hear the sounds. The
Rev. Charles Cravens, well known as a highly
intelligent and liberal minded universalist minister,
made the "invisibles a call, and unlike most men
of his profession treated the subject with the most
commendable and manly candor, whatever might
have been his private views in regard to the
matter.

The son-in-law of a very witty man, whose
common appellation was "Uncle Millard," and who
had previous to his desease lived in my native
village, called at our rooms one morning to see if he
could obtain any word or communication from him.
"Uncle Millard" had been about five years in the
spirit world, and was a quaint and quizzical character. He was indeed a wonder in his off-hand puns
and jokes, and having been personally acquainted
with him while he lived in our place, I naturally

felt some interest in what he might say to his son-in-law, who had come to speak with him. Seating ourselves in a circle about a large table at the usual hour in the morning, I was personally requested by the gentlemen to inquire for the spirit of "Uncle Millard."

Partly therefore to gratify Mr. Drake—for that was the man's name—and partly for my own satisfaction I inquired:

"Is the spirit of Mr. Millard present?"

After a moment's delay the medium's guardian replied:

"He is not now here, but we have called him and he will be here soon."

We waited patiently for eight or ten minutes when the sounds indicated a call for the alphabet and the following question was quickly propounded:

"What do you want of a fellow whom you thought had gone to perdition?

L. MILLARD."

Mr. Drake now attempted to ask a mental question. Waiting for some seconds he got no reply. At last the spirit said, in a manner somewhat hurried and as if endeavoring to decipher his thoughts:

"Why don't you tell what you mean, what do you set there trying to find an idea for?"

"Will you tell me when you died?" inquired Mr. Drake.

After hesitating again- for some little time, as if in doubt whether to answer or not, the spirit said:

"When you ask me a reasonable question I will answer. What is the use of inquiring when a man died whilst talking to him?"

When Mr. Drake had concluded his inquiries, I naturally had a desire to continue the conversation and so I asked:

Q. "Brother Millard, did you find things as you expected to in the spirit world?"

A. "When you tell me, young man, what *I did expect*, I will be better prepared to answer. As to whether it was painful to die, or pass from the earth-body, I can only say, no. But the change which I experienced was a curious turn in events, for it took me nearly a week to find out what I was doing."

Q. "Is your wife with you?"

A. What is the use of a wife to such an inquiring fellow as I am?"

Q. What is your occupation in spirit life?"

A. I am trying to spiritualize the more material elements of my mind, and I engage in all sorts of mental jangles to secure the knowledge I need."

Q. "Would you like to return to earth again?"

A. "I am as near the earth as I desire to be, and sometimes a little nearer."

The "sounds" were now becoming somewhat indistinct, and so I inquired:

"Can you not rap differently—louder?

"How different," was the reply, "I have only a *faucet* to open and shut, to become boisterous, if that's what you want."*

Loud and distinct sounds were now heard upon the table and floor, resembling the strokes of a man's fist against a board or door. These continued for some moments, but gradually diminished in force and died away to their usual capacity, and then ceased altogether.

After a brief social conversation which occurred among the members of the circle, the spirits again called for the alphabet, when the following touching and beautiful communication was transmitted to Mr. O. Maynard, who was a stranger to the medium, and a gentleman living in the vicinity of Le Roy:

"Brother, your Son and Father are both here with me. Father tells me to say to you, that M. and I are just as anxious to communicate, as you are to have us.

Father is your constant guardian. M. often impresses your mind with happy thoughts. We are all trying to develope a medium near you, for we would like to speak with you more frequently, that you might realize our presence when we are near.

We sometimes stand in a group above you and sing together to quiet your spirit, and invite it onward and upward to meet us in the Spheres of Love, where discord is unknown.

*Uncle Millard was sometimes in the habit of drinking too freely, hence the pun on a faucet.

Your M. is a bright and beautiful spirit.   He
says, "tell Father, it was hard for me to leave the
earth in the first bloom of manhood, but nothing
now would tempt me to return and assume or re-
sume the outward form again.   Still I wish that I
could speak to you as of yore, that you might hear me
and realize my presence, nor longer mourn my body's
decay, for I have a much more perfect one here.

When you weep, my kind father, let it be for
joy that you have a happy spirit Son, in a world
where death is unknown, and where he awaits with
joyous anticipation the time when he can meet and
welcome you to his immortal home.

Brother, I have rapped these thoughts just as
he uttered them, thinking it would gratify you.
Now one word from me.   We are altogether united
in one home, and when one comes to you the others
respond in spirit.

I am your ever-loving sister,

MARY MAYNARD."

Upon another occasion at one of our sittings in
LeRoy the following pathetic message was received.
The gentleman to whom it was addressed had been
for some twenty minutes or more occupied in making
mental inquiries in regard to his spirit friends, their
age at death, the length of time they had been in
the immortal realm, and many similar questions, all
of which he affirmed were correctly answered, when
suddenly a call for the alphabet—five raps—was
given, and the following lines, purely from the heart,
were quickly imparted to the recepient:

"I do not believe I have given you the dates correctly. Adeline says I have not, but I have done the best I could.

I know, Dear Father, that you no longer believe you have entirely lost your Gennett, but you do not realize my nearness as I wish you might. I wish you could feel my arms encircling your neck, and when you are unhappy hear my spirit whisper words of angel comfort and love. I would that you, my Father, could see me in my home in the refined atmosphere of our celestial realm. You would hardly recognize my shadowy form. I still love my dear Father and Mother above all else, and am always happy to have them know that I am near, for then I feel that they are near me.

Jonathan Miller is your guardian, but Adeline and I often impress your mind with a sense of feeling and thought.

I shall always make myself known to you whenever I can.

Good by, my kind Father and good gentle Mother, your daughter leaves with you her spirit love.

GENNETT MILLER."

Upon another occasion an old gentleman, whose hair was a fleece of whiteness, received the following sympathetic lines:

"I am glad to be able to speak with you once more. Glad that I can tell you how happy I am, and how we all meet and recognize each other in spirit.   I often come with Lucy to your bedside at night and converse with you in thought.

Your loved friends of this life have everything ready for you when your spirit is fully ripened and prepared to come to us.

I wish I could make you realize our condition more fully, for then it would seem as though you were already with us. We always feel happier when one of our loved ones from earth join with us to receive the felicities of immortal life.

I was just speaking with Seth C.   He wishes me to say that he is here.

I must now say good by.   Angel friends have greeted you.

I am still as when you saw me last.

TREPHENA PIERCE."

CHAPTER XVII.

FRIENDLY ACQUAINTANCES. A LETTER FROM HOME. SICKNESS. A TOUCHING COMMUNICATION.

We remained in the village of LeRoy for about two weeks, giving sittings twice each day. Our *seances* were well attended throughout. Strangers from a distance, men of letters and captious critics, honest investigators and doubters of spiritualism, atheists, deists and theists, scientists, philosophers and religionists came betimes to witness the manifestations and commune with the spirits, many visited our rooms with sad doubts in regard to the immortality of the human soul, who soon became convinced of its truth, as tearful eyes and sorrowful looks too often attested.

During the time which we remained in the family of Mr. Chamberlin we were kindly cared for by the generous matron of the household, who spared no pains in her effort to please us and others, and who was ever mindful of the sweet influence of her spirit guides.

I

A letter received one evening brought me the unwelcome news of sickness at home. My mother was dangerously ill. Notwithstanding the interest which I felt in the advancement of the cause of spiritualism, and the satisfaction which I had realized in my individual experience and intercourse with the "invisibles," I was convinced of the necessity of at once returning home, in order to care for my mother during her illness, and for the purpose of appropriating my time to the business pursuits —of farming and building—in which I had been engaged, but which I had temporarily neglected.

Without delay therefore we closed our visit in LeRoy and immediately returned to Victor. I found my mother prostrate and in a most critical condition. Her life was indeed despaired of. She had had a physician to attend her, but no seeming benefit had resulted from the medicine which had been administered. Her fever which had raged with terrible violence for many day was still unabated.

What were we to do? I sat down in meditation; regarded every circumstance; saw that my mother was beyond recovery, unless something was done at once.

Said I, "I will inquire of the spirits."

I done so, and was told to be patient and watch her symptoms with care.

Miss Irish sat by her bedside and gave her such attention as the "immortals" adviced. We were all fearful of the result. The little medicine which she was taking, however, soon seemed to work a beneficial change.

In twenty-four hours she was evidently better. In four days from the time of our arrival from Le-Roy and wholly as a result of spirit direction and watchfulness, she was so far recovered as to be able to rise and set up in her bed to receive care and nourishment, and we were soon relieved of our anxiety by her almost complete restoration to health.

As my mother was seated near the medium one evening during her convalescence, the spirits called for the alphabet, when she received the following kind and touching message:

"My dear Mother, I have been by your side many times during your recent sickness for the purpose of rendering you all the aid I could, and I have felt it a pleasure to do so.* I love my mother with that fondness which you are aware I know better how to realize than to explain. I am often reminded of the many motherly kindnessess which it was your happiness to bestow upon my needs during the long-continued illness and suffering, which it was my lot to experience during the three years which closed my earthly career, and my spirit often bows in thankfulness for the soothing words of comfort, which it was your habit to use in dispelling the gloom and sadness which frequently overshadowed my thoughts as a result of fancied unkindness in others, or from hopelessness and despondency of mind engendered as a consequence

*The weather being mild and outside doors open the spirit's ingress and egress was easily accomplished.

of my condition; and now I would gladly return
that affectionate and kindly sympathy so often
given to alleviate my distresses, by comforting thee
in spirit as far as I am able.

My dear kind mother, your elder loved son is
with you in heart, and bids you be happy in the
knowledge that your life in the home of immortality
will be made joyous forevermore by a reunion with
us, your loved children, who have been prematurely
called away to dwell amid the resplendent scenes
of a higher world.

JACOB Y. WRIGHT."

My Mother's heart was made glad by the receipt
of the welcome words thus transmitted to her keeping and my own feelings were buoyant with emotions
of delight, when I considered my Brother's kindness
in conferring upon us, as he thus had done, the assurance of his safety in being, and of the certainty
of eternal life as appointed to the lot of all humankind:

On the twenty-sixth day of April, and soon
after my mother had so far recovered from her
illness as to be again able to sit up in her easy
chair, Miss Irish, knowing that my duties at home
required my constant attention, and feeling that her
own interests prompted her to continue on in her
mission, bade us adieu, and after visiting for a few
days in the family of a neighbor of ours who was
also a spiritualist, she went eastward to the City
of Troy, and thence eventually to New York, where
she resided as late as the year 1862, giving private
seances at her residence in twenty-second street.

Dear reader, I was never—as I have before re-marked—disposed to be over-hasty in matters of belief, but on the contrary was ever inclined to exercise a sort of reserved criticism in considering all theories, statements, propositions or revelations in regard to a future life. My mind naturally wandered in search of a definite knowledge of the conditions upon which any hypothesis or phenomena rested, and I believed only when all doubts were removed through the acquisition of that positive testimony which the intellect—ever wary—could summon to its aid and approve.

I had now so far advanced in my investigation of the subject of spiritualism, pushing my efforts to that extreme limit of detailed research and examination that the evidence of its truth overwhelmed my objections, and I *knew* that invisible beings lived and communicated with men.

Day after day and week after week I had listened to the rappings, had written scores of alphabetic messages with my own hand, had interrogated the spirits without reserve upon any and all questions, at any and all times. I was no longer in doubt as to the continued existence and identity of my deceased Brother and Sisters and other loving friends, and I was now better satisfied, owing to the many dreams and visions which it had been my happiness to realize in previous years, that my Brother not only held some silent, secret relationship to my earth-life, but that he was instrumental in the production of my most singular *interior* experience.

Through the mediumship of Miss Irish and in my

presence the spirits had delivered to many an inquirer, thoughts the most beautiful, sentiments the most sympathetic, ideas the most enticing and acceptable. All mental questions were answered with accuracy and truth, where questioning was not *too long pursued.* The spirits evinced wondrous wisdom, as well as deep cupidity. They were kind and gentle in their words, but when closely criticized, usually foiled the purpose of the investigator by "sweet words" and "artful dodging" in the make up of their answers to interrogatories, or else for some reason to us inscrutable, they would refuse to communicate altogether— especially with some persons—and would remain entirely silent.

The more I saw of the physical manifestations, the better was I convinced that the angel world chose its instruments or mediumistic agents without regard to the moral characteristics which they personally represented. In other words, the principles of morality and association, as understood by us, became wholly anomalous in the light of immortal life. This was to me a most singular feature in the evidences presented from the other world, and as a consequence of my education and the teachings of society, one which I could not with pleasure advocate or maintain; yet with all I had no means of disproving the righteousness of such a condition of things as pertaining to life in the spirit realm.

"It is true," thought I, "that the law of wisdom is not the law of goodness, any more than the law of propriety is the law of morality; hence it may be a wise and universal privilege with spirits to be wholly free from our ideas of moral contamination and vicious contact. Indeed, the very acts which we consider to be noble and virtuous, may by them be regarded in a very different light, and as only appropriate to the conditions of earth-life."

Jesus said in answer to the inquiring and unsatisfied Sadducees—recognizing by inference the then existing marriage laws—that in the spirit they "neither married, nor were given in mariage."

This is to us a marvelous revelation. If spirits do not marry in heaven we may look for a great change. But not more wonderful was this disclosure of the Great Master, than was the announcement that:

"I am come to send fire on the earth."

"Suppose ye that I am come to give peace on earth? I tell you, nay, but rather division."

"For from henceforth there shall be five in one house divided, three against two, and two against three."

"The Father shall be divided against the Son, the Son against the Father; the Mother against the Daughter, and the Daughter against the Mother." All in justification of heaven's righteous law.

Then again, in Luke, chapter 16, verses 29 and 30, he advises the separation of a man from his parents, wife, children and all wordly goods, as a commendation to present happiness and future peace.

The methods of spiritualism, the idea of promiscuity, of deliverance in falsification, of contradictory communications, of evasion by artifice in well-worded replies to questions, and by the cloak of *mystery* as employed in many ways, are not more surprising than the utterances of the wise christian master as related in the four gosples, and instead of tending to demonstrate the existence of ignorance and wickedness as pertaining to the future life, are incontrovertable proof of the possession of *designing knowledge*, which is exercised by the "invisibles" as well in their own defense, as in derision of our weakness and presumption.

Miss Irish had been in our family better than two months, I had set with her in private and in public circles during the entire period, had listened to the rappings both by day and night, when the medium was awake and when she was asleep.*

I had studied the nature of the manifestations without stint or hinderance, and the evidence of the truth of spirit communion which I had received completely forbade denial. They had in every particular fulfilled their original promises with me and mine, and notwithstanding they had attempted a *Coup d'etat* upon my home-found attachments, I was less inclined to complain when I realized that delight which a true showman always feels when his efforts are crowned with financial success, for in that particular the invisibles had really proved themselves to be my happy friends.

.

*The medium had occupied a bed in a large chamber, while myself and. wife slept in a curtained grotto at one side of the room.

CHAPTER XVIII.

PERSONAL AFFAIRS. MY FATHER'S DEATH.
ANGEL GUARDIANSHIP. MOVE TO
MICHIGAN.

The domestic circumstances under which I struggled for several years subsequent to 1861, were not as pleasant in many particulars as I could have desired. The many demands made upon my time and energies to supply the daily necessities of a double household, absorbed the greater part of my attention, and consequently for a considerable period I neglected more than I otherwise should have done, the further contemplation of the many interesting subjects which come within the province of an enlightened spiritual philosophy.

Owing to money matters over which I had no control, and to an unfriendly spirit of opposition which was manifested toward me on account of the opinions which I entertained and advocated, I was for several years considerably oppressed for the necessary means—through want of remunerative employment—to supply the needful comforts demanded by our large family, the several members of which rested their expectations wholly upon my well-intended, though not always successful efforts. Hence it was that during much of the time I was obliged to abandon home and friends in order to find that occupation which would enable me to bring to them that indispensable maintainance which it is but just that all should possess and enjoy.

My Father was now nearing his eightieth year of age and had gone into decrepitude of both body and mind. During many years of his life he had, as I have before written, been associated with the Wesleyan Methodist denomination of christians as an officiating clergyman; but having long since retired from the regular ministry, and having also changed his views in many particulars concerning the subject of "religious precepts," and the various ideas which were entertained by the sects in regard to the immortality of the soul and the condition of the departed, he no longer retained the esteem or cherished regard of the self-sufficient adherents of "select theology," and being now in a great measure unable to defend himself against the ill-chosen words and slanderous epithets which were heaped upon himself and family, I was personally obliged to bear the burden of his abuse, until the close of his earthly career which took place in his eighty-sixth year of life.

Thus I suffered much pain and anxiety on his account during the decline which terminated in his disease, and when he had gone to that sphere of existence where nature's unseen populations dwell in wisdom and happiness, I was more joyous in my reflections concerning his condition, knowing him to have passed through a terrible ordeal of sickness and suffering, and feeling assured as I certainly did, that his spirit was now comparatively free from all distress and annoyance of the outward world.

However, when he had gone I could not help cherishing a sense of indignity toward those who had misrepresented or derided his name, for by a providence in his nature, he was eminently good of heart, as honest as man was ever made, and *cherished no thought of evil*. He was a kind and indulgent parent, an obliging neighbor, a wise adviser and sociable companion, and to those who sought to malign his character, in old age, because of his belief in free thought and spiritual intercourse I can only accord the applicable poetic sentiment that,

> "He who lives and does aright,
> May soonest claim his manly might."

During all my trials, troubles and wanderings which extended over a period of some fifteen years, it was never my satisfaction to neglect a just regard for the dear friends, my Brother, Sisters, and others who had climbed the high mount of everlasting life, and were enjoying the sublime solitudes of the infinite, interior realms of nature; and many and many a time was it my pleasure to ask, with a full heart and in reticent prayer, for guidance and counsel in

relation to the duties and responsibilities which
devolved upon me, and as often was I convinced
of the nearness and watchful care of the unremitting
guardianship of the Brother whom I had loved.

Upon one occasion he came to my bedside near
the morning hour, while the full round moon with
its silver face "yet led in the chase of the glowing
stars," and gently waking me from a deep and
dreamless slumber, by an electric shock, whispered
in my mind these words: *Go—to—the—window—my
Brother*, whereupon following his advice I arose from
my bed, and walking quietly to the window which
was open, I looked out upon the yard in front
of our dwelling, which was surrounded by large
sugar maple and cherry trees, and which was also
set here and there with variagated shrubbery and
flowers. A large number of pieces from the previous
days washing had been laid out upon the green
grass to dry. I knelt down by the window under a
sort of impulse derived from anxiety and a love
of nature, as I thought, and was looking up at the
azure firmament in silent admiration of the
greatness and grandeur exhibited in the display
of unnumbered worlds, while at the same time
thinking of the strange words which had
come from my cherished Angel Guardian, when
suddenly I observed a person stealthily stepping out
from behind a cluster of lilac bushes. Stooping down
he immediately began to gather to his arms the
various articles of individual wearing apparel which
were laying about upon the open ground in front
of my position. I at once comprehended the reason

of my having been called to the window, and as soon as I saw that the thief had fully committed himself to his calling, by having taken nearly all he could carry, I spoke in a very gruff manner and said:

"What on earth do you intend to do with those clothes?"

In the suddenness of his fright, he dropped his selected burden, and ran as if impelled by a shock of terror to the gate which he had fastened open. Hurriedly following the roadway in a northerly direction, the sound of his rapidly retreating footsteps soon died away in the distance, and all was still.

Thus I was made conscious of the attentive watchfulness and guardian care of one whom I had loved, and who in silence seemed still to feel an interest in protecting me from the unscrupulous hand of the midnight marauder. As I returned to my bed I found that wakefulness held its own in my behalf, and as the quietness of the hour was suggestive of serious thought, I wandered in reflection concerning the singular event which had just occurred. Thinking to myself, I said:

How strange it is that an invisible being can accomplish so much. I felt a slight shock as if my hand had held the wire connected with a galvanic battery, and simultaneously with my waking, and ere my faculties were fully aroused to consciousness, some one seemed to speak audibly in my mind, saying: *Go to the window, my brother.* Then all was silent and still. I went to the window as directed;

the bright stars were twinkling in the immeasurable distance: the brighter moon was wending her way toward the western horizon, and not even a zephyr moved amid the branches of the trees. It was pleasant to look out upon the shadows of the night, and I felt sorrowful as I contemplated the wonders of the heavens.

But the thief—what of him? Elated by his expectations he suddenly came, stealthily attempted to clutch our meager supply of underclothing, was defeated, and hastily ran away. Wherefore am I a novice in the study of the Spiritual Philosophy? Could I forget an angel Brother's kindness in saving my family from the toils of a vicious enemy? Even the sly and secretive thief was blessed by the timely interference of a being of the inward life. Our little washing was saved, and the mind that sought to benefit itself by villany was mortified by defeat and a consciousness of self-degradation in attempting to commit an inexcusable crime.

"What," thought I, continuing my contemplations, "what a commentary on the opposition to a belief in spiritual intercourse and the guardianship of unseen watchers. I wonder where my Brother was when he gave me the warning; where did he first discover the thief, and how long did he watch ere I was notified of his intentions. I could not see my Brother, yet I realized that he was near and desirous to do me and mine a generous favor. If spirits are thus careful of our just interests, and this event would seem to indicate that they are, then certainly they not only still love us, but must be conditioned in life somewhere *not far away*."

Thus I reasoned with myself until the light of the morning sun illuminated the eastern sky, when I arose from my bed at an unusually early hour, having been made wiser by my experience, and realizing a feeling of deep and lasting satisfaction as well as thankfulness, for the practical demonstration of spirit protection and care which had thus been exhibited toward me and mine.

My Father's death occurred in the month of September eighteen hundred and sixty-seven, and I immediately thereafter resolved to sell the real estate and personal effects belonging to our family and settle in the West. I had resided in Ontario County, in the State of New York, from my boyhood, and while I felt a strong reluctance to leaving my old home and the many happy surroundings of my younger days, it nevertheless became my settled ·conviction that I should better my circumstances by so doing. Hence in obedience to the opinion which I had thus formed, I sold the property which we possessed at private and public sale, and in the early spring of the year following my Father's demise, I journeyed to the West and located in the village of Middleville, in Barry County, Michigan, where I found and purchased a comfortable home, and quietly took to farming as a means of support.*

*The Author has been thus particular in speaking of the fact of his change of residence, for the reason that the events which soon after took place, and which were the cause of the development of his mind in Clairvoyant perception, are deemed of much importance in this connection.

CHAPTER XIX.

MONEY. ITS REWARDS. A VOICE.

PLANCHETTE.   HEARING IN SPIRIT.

Life is a turmoil at best, and he who succeeds in making a completence, adds as well to his cares as to his comforts. Some people are inclined to think that to be possessed of riches is to be made happy; whereas, in truth, wealth produces contention, augments our responsibilities, and rather increases our arrogance and the general tendency to a domineering and selfish disposition, than aids in augmenting our joy, or in building up the principles of honor, honesty, goodness or personal benevolence.

The mind naturally yearns to possess independence, and to be free from those corroding influences which cause distress, annoyance and unhappiness. To obtain wealth is therefore made a needful struggle, since it secures to us in a measure that desirable freedom from the abuses and sufferings engendered by poverty, which two-thirds of all mankind most reluctantly endure. The mandate of the financial world is imperative, and notwithstanding money brings its cares, the pursuit of life's greatest blessings are involved in the headlong and inordinate "grasp for gain," which is everywhere displayed in the trade, traffic, and industry of men.

When I had reached my new home in the West, where my family still reside, I found myself among strangers, with whom, as such, there could not exist that familiarity which I had enjoyed with lifetime neighbors and acquaintances in the place of my nativity. With a sufficient competency, however, to make my family comfortable, and with the income from the various products of our farm, which consisted of nearly two hundred acres of arable land, I felt that we could live and enjoy life in the light of greater domestic happiness and independence than we formerly had done, and although our social privileges were for a time more limited than previously, still this I regarded as a decided advantage, in so far that my family were relieved of the ordinary unpleasant gossip so apt to be on the wing in country towns, and of that overdone familiarity in social intercourse which is the fault of many people in village neighborhoods.

Thus as I contemplated my situation I began to realize the important fact that the buoyancy and vivaciousness which had characterized my experience in my younger days, was but too surely departing, while the more sober and reflective moods of mind, so peculiar to those advanced in years, came slowly creeping on. I could also see that I was drawing nearer to the *inward* condition of life. The silent *promptings* and *impressions* received from my guardian Spirit Brother, came into my mind with greater clearness and precision, and I felt that I was leading, so to speak, a "charmed existence" in the fullness of psychologic protection, direction and counsel.

Devoting most of my time to the fulfillment of the many duties which pertained to the proper cultivation of my farm, I would occasionally wander alone through the woods, with my fishing rod or gun, in search of the beautiful fish which abounded in the clear running streams, or the wild game which existed in great abundance along the Thornapple River, and throughout the forests in the vicinity of our home.

Sometimes, when weary I would set down to rest on the banks of this noble stream, and contemplating the sublime magnificence of nature's wondrous works, as they lay spread out in all the perfection of crude and unmolested creations around me, I could but inwardly exclaim:

Oh, God! Thy masterly wisdom is the source of my *joy*, yet equally the cause of my *sorrow*. The clear flowing waters at my feet dance and sing as they pass along, and the echo of their murmurings is heard like the chirping of the birds in the branches of the trees—a sad and solemn echo, productive of both joy and heartlessness. The tall, dark pines shake their green locks in the wind, and the gentle zephyrs lift the pendant leaves of the silver-aspen, with the tiny fingers of meek and gentle love.

The squirrels caper about among the limbs of the hollow oaks; the wild duck watches the interests of her little family as she glides along on the deep waters of the river in search of food; the quit, quit, of the wandering turkey, comes up from the distance and sounds on the ear, while the rust-ling of the hazel bushes not far away indicates the approach of the swift-footed deer and her agile fawn.

A yellow-hammer hacks away at the decayed trunk of an old standing elm, while within the scope of hearing the splash of the playful mink is heard as he plunges into the fretful current of the passing waters from the body of an old fallen ash. Above and far away in the sky, a grey eagle and a hawk ride the flowing stratifications of the air, with the ease and grace of the trancient clouds, peering down upon the beautiful landscape below with all the pride of high-minded success. The evening stars begin to glimmer, sending their flickering light down through the openings among the giants of the forest.

Thus upon one occasion I mused as I rested all alone toward the evening hour, on the green bank of the Thornapple River some three miles from my present home. I had wandered during the after part of the day with my gun in hand in search of wild game, and having a heavy burden of Teal and squirrels to carry, I had reposed in silent reflection beneath the shade of an over-hanging maple. While thus reclining I had wandered in thought over many a scene in life, until through weariness, and thinking I had unconsciously to myself induced

a condition of deep mental abstraction, when all at
once some one from behind me suddenly exclaimed
BROTHER, with impressive emphasis.

I immediately arose to my feet in the greatest
surprise, and finding no one near, I could only wonder at the singularity of the occurrence.

"A voice," thought I as I reflected, "it was
plain and distinct, and the word Brother was uttered
as if with a desire to surprise me. I wonder what
it all means."

As I recovered from the little excitement which
the suddenness of the event had occasioned, I inadvertantly ejaculated:

"That's a nice trick! I guess my Spirit Brother
thinks I am tarrying too long in the woods, and
that I had better be hastening home, or else he
wants to let me know that he is near, and that he
watches me in my rambles. I am satisfied that it
was him, it was so characteristic of his mischievous
ways."

Thus contemplating what had happened and
feeling my vital strength renewed as a consequence
of the rest which I had enjoyed, I swung my game
over my shoulder and taking my gun in my hand,
plodded along the winding pathway or "Indian trail"
by the river side, and soon reached our rural
dwelling.

During the Fall of 1868 my family were anxious that I should send for that mysterious little
instrument called Planchette, which was then exten-
sively advertised throughout the country, and was
for sale in nearly every city and village in the land.

Thinking that we might possibly enjoy its use, or that our supplications for spirit communion might be heard and thereby rewarded with satisfaction, I enclosed the needed amount for its purchase to a New York manufacturer, and soon received the precious little prize, which came nicely done up in a paper box. I immediately took it home where it underwent a most thorough inspection, and became not only the cause of laughter and amusement, but as well of many doubts and uncertainties in reflection.

My wife, more amused than gratified, remarked:

"I really don't believe it amounts to much."

My sister said:

"I don't see what there is about it."

My mother thinking silence preferable to remark, smiled, but said nothing.

When a thorough examination had been made, and Planchette had undergone a rigid criticism at the option of the various members of our family, the general desire seemed to be in favor of a trial of its capacities, and it being in the evening, I together with my wife sat down by a small table, and placing our hands upon it, patiently waited for nearly two hours, wishing for some demonstration, but without any definite result. After some general conversation in regard to our unsuccessful effort, I retired for the night, disappointed and discouraged, thinking that our little three legged ornament would be likely to prove a total failure, that our spirit friends were inclined to ignore its use, and that I had probably lost my investment.

When another day had passed, however, and the twilight of the early morning began to settle down upon the shades of night, we again yielded to the templation of trying the efficiency of our new and singular instrument. We waited and waited, quietly sitting by our table until something more than an hour had passed, when all at once as if by the influence of magic the deceptive truant of undiscoverable motive power began to dodge about as if inflated both alike with zeal and intelligence.

Planchette moved. Why did it move? What could be the cause? It answered all the mental questions asked by myself and others with correctness, sometimes with captiousness. *Who* answered the questions, was a ligitimate inquiry, and one which it became necessary to wisely consider. Certainly no member of my family wished to be deceived, and as for myself I desired only to *know the truth.*

Partly from distrust, but more from fear, my wife had abandoned the hope of receiving anything satisfactory from the spirits, by its use, as a result of the first trial; hence, the burden of our anxiety and expectation in regard to its employment had fallen to my confidence and care, and I became the "witch" in whose hands the "three legged stool of satan"—as it has been abusively denominated— moved, and *my* mediumship was supposed to be established.

Some said Planchette was a nuisance. It was unreliable, insincere and irresponsible. I regarded it as a great curiosity; and judging from many of its

movements, and especially from its reluctance to
speak freely and frankly as mortals speak with
mortals, I was not in the least surprised that people
should sometimes become frightened and superstitious from witnessing its antics, and ejaculate,
"humbug," "mystery," and other similar unmeaning
phrases.

Planchette is a most artful object, thought I.
It has a pasteboard constitution and loves to be well
ornamented. It has neither mind nor consciousness,
yet it often bows with significance. It manifests wondrous intelligence, but it possesses no visible mental
organization. It writes prose, and it writes poetry,
but the author is unseen. The *savants* are doubtful of its veracity. They say it contradicts its own
assertions, and becomes inorderly. The neighborly
minister says that it is the work of Satan, and to
him is accorded the most unlimited power. Thus
under the pretense of doubt or through assumed
fear of evil, they abandon the field of investigation
with self-imposed derision, and an unhappy acknowl-
edgment of their inability to disclose a mystery, solve
a problem of interest, or treat a marvelous subject
with just and becoming consideration.

Persistency is said to be the source of success.
Some people would have laughed most heartily at
my unremitting earnestness and the determined
attention which I manifested in my effort to reach a
knowledge of the cause or causes involved in the
movements of Planchette. It being at a season
of the year when my time was not much occupied, I
pursued the subject of spiritual intercourse through

my little instrument with the greatest diligence and care.

I was zealous, eager, honest, sincere and candid in every effort and I resolved that since the spirits had condescended to manifest themselves intelligently through the use of my hand, that whatever might be the objection, I would go to the bottom of the enfolded *Garnee* of spirit demonstrations thus given if possible. A foreknowledge of the consequence of my persistency in the matter of my investigations, or of the sufferings which I was doomed to endure, would undoubtedly have caused me to desist, but ignorance we are told—and confession is no crime— is the cause of many lucky blunders, and as I could not foresee the result of a too great intimacy with the "invisibles," I continued asking for favors until the end of about three weeks, when as a consequence of continuous concentration of mind, I found myself a subdued subject of spirit-psychology.*

During the first two weeks I had written several beautiful communications, which were dictated by spirit friends, or those who claimed to be my spirit Brother and three Sisters. They were quite familiar and conversed with the various members of my family with unusual freedom. Numerous were the questions asked concerning the home of the spirit, the experience in spirit life of those whom we had loved, and the condition of being which they enjoyed. For several days this unreserved intimacy and

*The author is now satisfied that he was influenced to anxiety by the preconcerted design of spirits; whether that design was good or bad is a question which I shall leave for the reader to decide, when he has heard my story.

friendship continued, but after what will ever seem to me as a most remarkable reunion—in social inter-course—of the departed, with those still living in the relationships which pertain to mortal existence, after nearly a fortnight of conversational affability and kindly discourse between friends long separated, and upon an occasion when I was alone, and when least expected, my spirit guide very kindly advised me to desist from further freedom in gratifying the curious in matters pertaining to spirit communion, and coun-seled me to retire to my private room, and there receive such needful educational training and instruc-tion, as would enable me to write upon subjects of practical interest to mankind, and promising at the same time, that if I would do so, I should have aid in writing a work to be entitled the "Mas-tereon."

Previous to this time, however, and even during the third week of my experience with Planchette, I began to realize a singular sensation which seemed to pervade my entire nervous system, and was accompanied by a definite realization of hearing *in the mind.* Words, sentences and paragraphs were dis-tinctly articulated in this manner, and I soon discovered that they were given by a purely impressional or imparted process. They were uttered, articulated and enunciated to the consciousness of the soul, as perfectly as if delivered to the exter-nal ear by the oral sounds of the human voice, *and I knew that I was listening to invisible beings.*

The thoughts which came into my mind pro-ceeded from the *designed* reflections of my guardian

J

spirit, and I was satisfied that I was held in psychologic subjection to his imposed will, for their impartation. Thus I gradually entered the sphere of interior hearing or *clairaudience,** and casting

*Hearing in the spirit is truly a rare gift of mind, yet it has been possessed in various degrees of perfection by several persons in past ages.

Daniel, the Magian Prophet, affirms that he spoke with the dead in the condition of trance, for he says Dan., 9th chap. and 9th verse: "Yet heard I the voice of his words, and when I heard the voice of his words, then was I in a deep sleep, on my face, and my face toward the ground."

It is stated in Acts 9th chap., 7th verse that Peter heard a voice which advised him, and gave him confidence.

After opening the prison doors the angel admonished the prophets to "Go, stand and speak in the temple all the words of this life," Acts, 15th chap., 20th verse.

Socrates is said to have conversed with Demons.

Zoroastor communed with celestial spirits.

Homer spoke with spirits from childhood.

Ignatius, Bishop of Antioch, is said to have "heard the Angels sing."

Christ conversed with Moses and Elias on the mount.

Mozart, the great musical composer, more impressible in mind than clear in spirit hearing, says: "My thoughts come streaming in upon me, whence or how I cannot tell."

M. Nicoli, in a narrative which he has given concerning things which he witnessed—not knowing himself to have been in psychologic trance of his own mental faculties—says:

"About four weeks after their—the phantasmagorical spiritual personages—first appearance, I began also to *hear them speak*. They sometimes conversed among themselves, but more frequently they directed their conversation to me. Their speeches were commonly short, and never of an unpleasant tenor. Several times I saw beloved and sensible friends of both sexes, whose addresses tended to appease my grief, which had not wholly subsided. These consolatory speeches were in general addressed to me when I was alone; sometimes, however, I was accosted by these consoling friends whilst in company, *even while real persons were speaking with me*."

Swedenborg makes the following statement in regard to the speech of Angels with men in his work entitled "Arcana Celestia:"

"The speech of an Angel or a Spirit with man is heard as sonorously as the speech of a man with a man; yet it is not heard by others who stand near, but by himself alone; the reason is because the speech of an Angel or Spirit flows first into the man's thought and by an internal way into his organ of hearing and thus moves that from *within*; but the speech of man with man flows first into the air, and by an external way into his organ of hearing and moves it from *without*. Hence it is that the speech of an Angel and of a Spirit with man is heard in man, and because it equally moves the organs of hearing, that it is also equally sonorous; that the speech of an Angel and of a spirit flows down even into the ear from within, was evident to me, from this that it my Planchette aside, as no longer needful to my use —it having simply served to fix my attention and concentrate my mental faculties until I became the subject of spirit influence and control—I could sit in quietness in my chair and give expression to the words, ideas and conversation of unseen beings.

While in this incipient condition of development in *mental hearing*, it was my pleasure one day, after I had endured much anxiety and suffering as a subject of mesmerism, to receive the wondrous communication herewithin next given, and which was delivered extemporaneously in the presence of my family as the thoughts and words were uttered *in my mind*, while my sister, who acted as Amanuensis, gave them to writing as fast as expressed.*

also flows into the tongue, and excites in it a slight vibration, but not with any motion as when the sound of speech is articulated by it into words by the man himself."

Then again he says:

"The discourse or speech of Spirits conversing with me, was heard and perceived as distinctly by me as the discourse or speech of men. Nay; when I have discoursed with them, when I was in company also with men, I also observed that as I heard the sounds of man's voice in discourse so I heard also the sound of the voice of Spirits each alike sonorous."

The author of this volume does not agree with Swedenborg as to the use of the term "sonorous"—which signifies "loud sound"—in its application to "spirit hearing." Although utterance *in the mind* which comes down *through the top of the head*, is identical with hearing produced by the vocal sounds of the human voice and the impression is the same to the sense of consciousness, still it is evident that spirit hearing is rather the result of the silent precipitation and evolution of thought from invisible mind by a *diaphonic* process which is really unsonorous, than by any method which involves the idea of sound.

*Mr. A. J. Davis committed himself to utterance as provoked through spirit cotrol while *entranced* and totally unconscious of external things during his early experience as a seer. The writer on the contrary loses no sense of external consciousness while in the delivery of words, ideas or theories from the inner world, and is not commonly given to trance during daylight hours.

CHAPTER XX.

A REMARKABLE MESSAGE.

Oh, come to the Spirit Land, my Brother, and in imagination walk with me, hand in hand, where suns and systems glide onward with unerring precision through the open *Horlanzava** of all-abounding space. Observe the countless tribes and nations of diversified beings, immortalized wanderers in the hazy depths of a universe without end, the offspring of innumerable planets, assembled in the sky, and winging their flight with orderly design along the endless circle of *Via-lactea*, in obedience to Divine Command.

The open vista of the broad blue vault of heaven is our eternal home. All space is lit up with livid and undying light to bless the dwellers who inhabit the kingdoms of immensity, and none may ever mea-

*In the wisdom of the spirit the boundlessness of space becomes an unhappy subject of thought.

sure or comprehend while time shall last the full extent of the beauty, grandeur or holiness of creation; neither the extent of that awarding power which seeks abandonment in the system of nature, for the promotion of all good, as effected through the action of abrasive laws.

We of the spirit, although organically formed, move through space like the fleet lightning in our passage from place to place. In our journeyings in the future, my Brother, we may gaze upon innumerable worlds, and cancel our claim to personal happiness as well as sorrow, by the acquisition of knowledge and the sight of scenes more blessed, more *terrible*, than all which belong to, or have been associated with the growth and progress of the earth in past ages.

Looking down upon foreign worlds, the sage *Amaana*, or traveler in immensity, may see and contemplate the sublime meaning announced in the gracious molestations of nature, or represented in its material labyrinths.

Oh, what a pleasure to gaze upon the countless coiling rivers, which beautify and adorn the surface of revolving orbs, as they flow onward filled with teeming life over continents and hemispheres, many times larger than those of our mother planet. Then again, behold the many tribes, races and nations of human beings, which people the diversified spheres hung out in the broad blue heavens; how strangely formed; how variously conditioned. These are the subjects for an eternal lifetime of contemplation and study, rewarding the efforts of the soul with joyous satisfaction and knowledge. It is a source of *awful* delight, for the spirit to witness the plunging of mighty waters, as they descend the ragged steeps or couch beneath the time-worn precipice over which they fall with deafening roar; or as they foam under the terrible pressure of the maddened winds, as they chase the waves in fury over the surface of seas and oceans, whose extent it is absolutely horrifying to contemplate.

I have stood over the *Lahavien* sea on the planet Jupiter, and shaded my eyes in sorrow, as I gave my heart to the Infinite Spirit, in the troubled vision which I beheld while gazing far over her tumbling billows.

I have watched the glutted *Gcharleus* as they lay in mighty shoals along the terraced reefs, or pierced the silvery liquid with their massive, hacking horns in search of prey.

What think you, my Brother, of a marine monster so wondrous in its strength, and so singularly formed, as to be able to plough immense furrows in deep sand beds, at the bottom of oacens wherein it dwells, and cast the contents thereof in every direction by the use of its sinuous nose, its claws, and the rapid evolutions of its finless tail.

While standing up on the hights of *Himemeyon* I shrank back in terror as I reflected upon a scene which presented itself in the transparent depths of the sea, for below my position. A mighty, compact, moving mass of these wriggling, cumbersome monsters, fifteen hundred miles in length and sixty miles abreast, were wandering in migration through

the watery element at the base of a series of low
submarine ridges and were wallowing in the mud
and sand, and literally tormenting nature by their
hideous presence. No living creature dwelling within
the limits of that beautiful sea of tenciled waters is
able to withstand the furious power of these voracious animals.

When in the future we wander together in spirit,
my Brother, we shall be able to look upon the wondrous works of the Divine Creator, and behold the
sublime order which attends the development
of worlds and of universes, in the immeasurable
labyrinth of nature. We may then contemplate as
companions in eternity, the righteous law which holds
all matter in subdued action, determines the real
relationships existing between all things organically
formed, and substantiates the value and holiness
of Omnipotent Design.

When you depart from the earth, my Brother,
and come to dwell with me, we will *yellow* ourselves and go on a visit to the planet Mars. With
gay and joyous hearts we will quickly journey
thither. Well will we make the ethereal waters
smile. As we pass along we will drink of the
golden nectar of *Mekernellah* and sing the song
of the lost *Twarrvi*, a sweet though sorrowful
melody, expressive of the loneliness of the traveler
who journeys through space from world to world in
search of knowledge and happiness. With these it
is not infrequently the case that they become lost,
hopelessly lost to family, friends, kindred and all
former associations, and in their absence they are

known to linger, amid strange scenes and stranger
populations, in remotest regions of nature's immeasurable domain.

We will visit the Oacen fountain of *Sainomi* on
the planet Saturn, where the heated waters pour
forth in massive columns over a broad aera, boiling
and steaming heavenward with a rumbling roaring
sound like a mighty cataract. Returning in the season of planetary juxtaposition by a pleasant line
of travel, we will visit the magnificent temple of *Ye-
gehlenon* which is situated upon an ever-green isle in
the shining purple sea of *Gahjah* in the circle of the
tropics upon the planet Jupiter.

Upon this beautiful island, in peaceful contentment and quiet happiness, retire and rest in joyful
hope many of the aged people of the noblest race
who dwell in outward life within the broad circumference of our solar system. For some years previous to their departure to the charmed existence
which they inherit as immortal beings in the brilliantly illuminated atmosphere of their native world,
they retire betimes to the delightful seclusion of this
magnificent home.

We will make a journey to the far-clime beyond
the sparkling milky-way—in the future—and observe
the enormous *Hkneohenlenla* as it slumbers in peren-
nial repose.

We will visit the *Aufstkan* gardens of *Omitihi*
where time is employed in musical jubilation, and
spirits are instructed in the more exalted methods
which pertain to the proper enunciation of sweet and
harmonious sounds.

We will join the *Chklemlew* of *Meithasos* and learn the lesson of ample calculation as it is taught to the studious *Wahrvi* of that wondrous institution.

We will visit the sacred *Kunarlavun*, where we may behold the wise and highly gifted *Ghauvons*, who are employed in conditioning the "Holy Desires" of the "Just in Heaven," to nobler prospects in harmonious joy and accordant happiness in life.

We will visit the golden *Ahtaa Azalen*, where the lesson of individuality is taught in the greatest degree of perfection, and the mind is aided to the possession of the fullest knowledge in self-comprehension.

And lastly, my Brother, we will visit the wise and noble chief who rules the heavens above with unsubdued and masterly will, that we may contemplate the grandeur and perfection of the celestial government of the immortal world.

Will you come with me, my Brother, never will I be so happy as when you come to dwell with me in the home of the spirit."

When I had finished the delivery of this message which occupied nearly an hour on four different evenings, the subject being recommenced on each successive occasion—by the guardian spirit—exactly at the point of suspension on the previous night, and as if without reflection, I could only exclaim in the deep thankfulness of my own heart.

"Oh; how marvelous, how inscrutable are the laws of mind. Here sitting in my own dwelling, together with my family, in the happy enjoyment and quietness of domestic life, I am enabled to listen with freedom to the voice of my spirit Brother *as he speaks in audible utterance in my mind,* and conveys his ideas, thoughts and sentiments to me as the gift of his wisdom and love.

Oh ; how strange that I should hear his "still small voice" speaking to me so plainly, so distinctly. Even as when in boyhood twenty-five years ago we rambled together on the old farm, gathering the fruit of the trees as it fell dislodged from the pendant branches by the force of the autumn winds, or as we lingered in favorite haunts for the purpose of sport, play and pastime—so speaks he with me now, inviting me to reflection concerning that exalted life which it was his to prematurely inherit.

Is it possible, thought I, that I can "speak with the dead," and yet all the world be groping in darkness concerning the subject of immortality. Men neither know that they live after death, nor whither they are tending as beings of consciousness, activity and contemplation. They look up into the sky, admire the sublime beauty of nature's handiwork; yet withall, they know not of the home of the "immortals," nothing of the kind friends, the generous kindred who have departed in silence to be seen no more.

Men are struggling in their own minds to solve the great problem of spirit existence. They preach ; they pray; they weep; yet nature opens not the door of her inner temple to the children of earth.

Now and then a Daniel, Ezekiel, St. John, Swedenborg or a Jacob Beohm, avow that they hear the voices of angels, or speak with the unseen inhabitants of the super-mundane world, but failing to clearly explain the phenomena which they claim to experience, or leaving the subject of their own realizations enfolded in clouds of uncertainty and doubt, they have left their meaning to be mis-interpreted and misconceived, and mankind, becoming superstitious over their unguarded and ambiguous statements, have wandered from a just understanding of those psychologic laws, which when wisely regarded, so readily and so clearly explain the many mysteries associated with the abnormal action of the human mind.

The more I reflected concerning what had passed, the more astonished I became. To converse with people about a matter which they did not and could not understand, I found to be a very useless expenditure of time, and one which was usually more productive of unfortunate results than of satis-faction or success.

The idea that I was spoken to by invisible beings who enunciated their words and sentences in my mind by a silent process, yet in a manner to be heard as mortals hear each other, and that I alone was the recipient of such hearing, was to me a source of astonishment if not of real distress, for I felt that to be solely endowed with such a gift, was so marvelous a feature in individual experience, that its possession could never become a cause for comfort or rejoicing under the prevailing influence of incredulity and dominating self-satisfaction in knowledge.

When I said to persons who sometimes conversed with me in regard to my condition, that my Brother's voice came to my interior hearing in plainest speech, that when in conversation with others, neighbors, friends, strangers, at home, on the street, in the cars, here and there and everywhere, I could hold communion with the departed, a smile, a shake of the head, or a shrug of the shoulder, announced the futility of all attempts to satisfy them concerning a truth which it was not their privilege to realize as I did, and I was hence convinced that "physical manifestations" were wisely given by the inhabitants of the spirit world to punish a willful skepticism and a pretentious righteousness among men.

CHAPTER XXI.

THE PRINCIPLE OF WILL.

Soon after the receipt of the beautiful communication presented to the reader in the previous chapter, the following singular thesis upon the subject of "The Principle of Will" was commenced and delivered extemporaneously, while my Sister and Nephew both at times acted the part of scribe, receiving and writing each word, sentence or paragraph as fast as uttered.

"The only way to learn the valuable lessons of wisdom, is to still the elements of inward strife, and seek the consolation of earnest thought and study. The merits of any cause, however just, may be jeopardized by hasty and willful action. The imperfection which is manifested in, and associated with all human affairs, is a result arising mostly from the impetuous exercise of the pertinacious principle of will. The mind becomes abased, or otherwise elevated in self-perfection, as surrounding influences fashion or control the will to conditions of good or evil. Sometimes the human mind becomes so biased as a result of local causes, under the instigation of will in misdirection, that life itself is rendered abnoxious, burthensome and inharmonious to the individual, and distress, discord and unhappiness, rather than the joy and felicity which results from evenness of mind, is the inevitable consequence.

The human mind is a microcosm in which the office of nature is more or less perfect, in conformity to pre-natal influences, subsequent circumstances, surroundings, individual habits and associations.

When the mind represents itself in goodness, justice or benevolence, the atomic substance of the brain tends to a convergance in the moral faculties in layered consistency, or in great uniformity and order of its seried conformations. The highly intelligent mind is often so closely bound by the ties of compact in its organic dependence, that the very words employed in speech are concentrated and combined in the smallest possible compass, with yet a force equal to a more loose and voluminous utterance.

The brain of man is so constructed as to unite the principle of Love and Will. Life is made permanent by this unseen union of positive and negative forces, and human consciousness—an inevitable outgrowth of their organic association—is a result productive of wisdom, which is knowledge, gained by observation, reflection or intuition, and which lives in memory, having its seat in the *focus* or centre of the mind.

Oviparous inter-communion is the righteous source of that *Mixte* of *Renezeun* elements, which when *Arteveed* in life, become the responsible cause of physical growth and mental expansion, and by slow degrees of the development of will. Mind is the seat of the most subtle will. Will is the centre of constantly increasing wisdom; and we cannot discover its origin, or the cause of its existence or operations. Will is the only thing which is wholly commonplace in the universe, as an all-pervading element of power, and yet which is utterly incomprehensible to the mind.

Mind is the only thing which can examine will, and will is the only thing which can control mind. Mind is the only power which possesses the attributes of ever-to-be continued expansion in all things pertaining to intelligence; yet mind may be delayed in its progress as a result of its dulness in perception or the inaptitude of its component faculties.

The principle of will is so subtle in its composition that the connexion between it and the mind is not and cannot be comprehended. Will is the only thing which cannot be analized, is the only thing which is to continue in control of the mind throughout eternities of time, and yet we shall never know the full extent of its power. Will is the only thing wholly at the mind's disposal, yet which controls the interests of the mind.

Will is a power which is ever to be dreaded, and comes from the great fountain of causation. As a Divine element will is the only all-abounding influence which works incessant changes in nature to

the building up and disorganization of worlds, and
the order and confusion of matter. Will is a mighty
engine of power, and combines the energies of destruction with the united elements of wisdom. The
principle of Infinite Will is an inconceivable agent or
combination of inscrutable forces, wandering at the
instigation of wisdom in the everlasting abuse and
correction of unlimited Deific creations. Will is the
motive power of Omnipotence, constantly moving all
matter in the universal *Jan-za* of space, and is the
active cause of the organization and disorganization
of worlds, universes and all material forms. Under
the force of Infinite Will suns and systems are
brought into being, continued in existence for an indefinite period, die, become confused, circulate
through the immensity of space in concentric circles
of commingling atoms, become resolved into order,
break into the formation of worlds, and bedeck the
blue expanse of heaven with newly unfolded stars
and planets, which persue the privilege of destiny
with a new and wondrous lease of life.

Will is ever at work in all departments of the
boundless universe of matter, is restless in its efforts,
builds up and destroys organic forms, by fashioning
congenial atoms into seried stratifications, and carry-
ing them back again into dissolution of their
aggregated particles. The will of the Omnipotent
Spirit adjusts and controls the endless dominion over
which he lavishes His kindly care; and the whole
organic temple of nature is corrected by this diffu-
sive principle under the promptings of Infinite
foresight.

Will is the only good yet mischievous power. It lingers on the confines of the great worlds of omnipotent creation, and yields to the orderly suggestions of Divine Wisdom. Will is a *yellow* principle, permeating and penetrating all matter. It exists in association with all atoms, is centralized and focalized in the organic structure of all forms, worlds, suns and systems.

We cannot reach by observation the movements or motions of the principle of will. Its combined activities are altogether inscrutable; yet its influence is everywhere present. Mind feels the contact of mind with mind through the force of will. By this approach we experience a sensation which either mars or pleases the feelings. The understanding is thus notified of that which is congenial or disagreeable, and conclusions are thus formed.

Will is the only principle in existence which is not clearly soluble by the mind's executive comprehension, and is the only thing which the mind may never fully fathom. Will is the Great Power which was the cause of the beginning of the present order of nature as exhibited in the universe, and in the far-future this all-prevalent principle, will undo all harmony in matter as expressed in the order and formation of worlds now existing in space, to the end that a higher and more perfect condition of Divine Order, Harmony and Law may exist.

When will is willfully operative it is the *Ultima-thule* of positive power. When it is tacitly active, it is the medium of combined commerce between everything in being. Will is a most perfect combination

of latent and eternal principles; is the most interior
of all elements; can never be destroyed; cannot be
coerced into permanent inactivity, or in any way
become lost to the wondrous purposes for which
it was primarily intended as the vehicle of combined
use and destiny. The principle of will is the productive cause of all *motion*. Matter is organized and
disorganized, is condensed and consolidated, or is
abrazed, volatilized and dispersed by its incessant
action. At the suggestion of wisdom, this all-con-
trolling principle wanders forth in its commercial
evolutions to build up or destroy planets, suns and
systems, nebula, and endless belts of stars; and in
its all-powerful grasp are held the countless orbs,
which gather around the Infinite centre of being,
and course throughout the ethereal realms of space,
with periods as diversified, and revolutions as sur-
prisingly rapid, as they are terrifying and inconceivable.

The principle of will is the only thing which is
entirely transitory in its characteristics, and yet
which is unfathomable to the mind or understanding.

Will is a most wonderful phenomenon. In its
universal relation to nature it supports and executes
the edicts of Divine Wisdom without rest or
neglect. Its action is perpetual. It moves in the
breeze; is terrible in the storm; maddens in the
waves; is pleasant in the sunshine, and genial in
the rippling stream. Will is the monitor which pre-
sides over intellectual consciousness. When guided
by wisdom it prompts the individual to the
performance of acts of justice and benevolence,

becomes subservient to the practice of worthy virtue and morality, and points the way to ultimate peace and happiness.

Will is the efficient law of a comprehensive system of use and beauty too vast to be understood by the mind of man, or fully known even to the evangels of light among the truly blessed in higher spheres of eternal life. Will reaches out into the unfathomable depths of time and space, is the active promoter of all life, seeks equality in nothing animate or inanimate, yet does the bidding of the Great Ruler of nature, with power, precision and tireless energy.

Will is a manifest expression of the only system of commingling forces in the wide spread universe, as emenating from the decisions of the Great Supreme Author. To Spirits, that power pervading the realms of matter most worthy of their contemplation, is the principle of will; and only when we come to understand the motives which abound in the deep secluded recesses of Infinite Wisdom, can we know of the practical operations of the yellow principle which we term will.

The most astounding influence of will is presented in the tremendous efforts of nature to accomplish the purposes involved in her continuous changes and destiny. In the principle of will there is uncertain and dreaded power. It is wicked in its wantonness, and obliging in its happy ways. It wanders in the destruction of the creations of its choice, and quietly gathers the broken fragments of mutilated forms and moulds them into new and

wondrous objects. Will has no love for the principle
of Life, neither desire in the qualification of Death.
Wisdom ever watcheth the motives of will in its
circuitous wanderings and mechanical evolutions in
the infinite regions of space, and in its subduing
strength holds it in neefdul subjection to timely
and considerate use.

Will is the agent of wisdom, but often abuses
the commands which it receives in the performance
of its duties.   The only record showing where the
Infinite Being dwells is found in the perambulating
worlds which fill the sea of immensity to repletion.
When the Omnipotent Father caused the domain
of nature to be studded with gems, he also caused
the principle of will to go forth on its mission
of everlasting perturbation, for the furtherance
of those purposes which pertain to the demands
of progressive law.

The principle of will in its manifestation is the
outspoken expression of the mind in its desires.
Will must ever conform to the bidding of its superior master wisdom; but may temporarily diverge
from the support of justice and become the servant
of selfish or unguarded use.

When the only thing designedly supervising,
which is wisdom, succeeds the only thing uncompre-
hended, which is will, then the final principle must
surely take the precedence of power, purpose and
responsibility. Will is in diversity of manifestation
in all time, in all places, and in all things; yet it is
ever the same in its ceaseless activity in the Divine
Economy of the universe, and in it there is no

quibbling cause; for wisdom in its supreme super-
vision gives that safety to all things in being which
is sure, steadfast and unalterable. The greatest
power which comes from God's Wisdom is his overwhelming goodness and all-embracing love; and the
holy system of mechanism abounding in the unlimited
realms of space, is founded upon these two chasten-
ing principles of Omnific Origin. To suppose our
Heavenly Father deficient in the means of controlling
for everlasting good, "The temple of his handiwork,"
would be to acknowledge a purpose lacking that
perfection and consistency, which his position and
relation to nature would imply.

To the thoughtful mind there is one only Infinite and Eternal Being, whose intentions are just,
whose motives are wise and well-timed, and whose
Great Heart embraces in its sublime strength, the
celestial seraph of the highest heaven, as well as the
less expectant intelligences, dwelling within the
confines of his broad domain.

God is a creator only through the force
of the action of Omnipotent Will. By and through
the energy of this ever restless principle, the
designs of the Infinite Being are carried into practical effect. Will sends its scintillations of motion
broadcast into the unfathomable depths of immensity,
and in the fullness of its corrective influence it yields
to no obstacle or objection. Will is the only source
of success to the plans of the Divine Architect, and
the only promise of safety ever given to intelligent
beings who live within the confines of the temple
of nature.

When the Father-mind of the universe caused the chaotic elements of the whole structure of the boundless universe of his pride and care, to unfold in beauty, order, form and harmony, from a state of inorganic abrasion and restless commingling insecurity, then was presented the most perfectly outspoken expression of the all-prevalent principle of Infinite Will.

The hope of mind in nature rests in the capacity of will. The safety and satisfaction of being reposes in the cautious purposes of wisdom. If will is rendered submissive, or is advised and directed by wisdom, then is wisdom inevitably the only safe and reliable guide to conditions of light, harmony and happiness in the individual, and the only responsible power acting as a Divinely Authorized Agent in the watchful protection of the incalculable interests, which abound in every department of creation.

When we contemplate the action of will as manifested in its devious wanderings, or as engaged in the performance of the sublime duties which pertain to its exalted mission, in the spheres of matter and the labyrinths of mind, we can only conclude that the general safety and eternal continuance of matter is certain, that it is fixed in its tendency to seek organic forms, and that the happiest results to all intelligent mind may be inferred as a consequence of such a wondrous and orderly resolution of force.

Will often presents features and phases of manifestation quite as absurd and unsatisfactory as

they are uniformly resultant of worthy effect. When
taken as a whole the demonstrations of will tend as
well to astonish and confound the intellect, trying
the confidence of the soul in its belief in the
permanency of nature, as to establish the certainty
of eternal order, goodness, justice and the stability
of Omnipotent Design.

Will is a principle which if unrestrained by
mind, or unguided by that wisdom which is ever
inseparable from its existence, would not only roam
at large with indiscreet and wanton force, but would
produce universal disorder, anarchy and confusion
throughout the boundless realms of space.

Wisdom is a gracious guard, a reliable guide, a
safe defense against every abuse and excess; for
although mind or matter may swerve from the point
of central attraction, from the highest good, from
fixed fealty to established law, yet they are sure to return again to the rule of just and righteous action,
under its imperative demands, and serve the best
purposes involved in their every natural use and inclination.

The will of the Infinite Being is alone represented in the _Pleonum_ power which holds the immeasurable universe in incessant toil and duty, and
in all its relations to matter and the ethereal elements of mind, it can only yield its insensate force
and ever active energies, to the interests dominating
in the watchful principle of wisdom, which in its
Omnicient capacity controlls all things in creation
with unerring precission for ultimate good.

Matter is not only bound to obey the commands

of wisdom as guided by its appointed agent will, but
will is obligated to perform the office of all contention
and strife in the limitless domain of nature. The
central element of power which we denominate will
can no more oppose the general purposes of wisdom,
than can wisdom suspend or destroy the needful
operations of will. The mental will is a sublime
phenomenon, and is a result of the combined active
relationships of the various faculties of the mind. Men
and women are the inheritors and responsible possessors of this wonderful principle, which is the servant of intelligence and which is as varied in the
characteristics of its manifestation, as individuals are
different in their physical appearance and constitu-
tional peculiarities. Some persons are in the exercise
of will for beneficial and worthy purposes, while
others are as earnest in effecting unwise and mischievous objects. Will can only serve that wisdom
which the mind enjoys and is able to make practical
in life. Will is not *identical*. It answers all demands. It serves the poor, and it serves the rich.
Aided by intelligence, without goodness, it becomes
ungenerous and serves a willful and wicked object.
Stimulated by want or prompted by views founded
in self-abasement and degradation, will becomes the
servant of utterly selfish motives, and seeks satisfaction in theft, murder and self-destruction. In pro-
portion as will is left without the guidance of wisdom,
in such ratio does it become annoying and objectionable through its hasty and unguarded manifestations.
To the wise man will is ever a blessing. It serves
him in reason; he holds its wanton inclinations in

check; he makes it his servant; he is its master.

Will enables the toiler to accomplish his task; it provides the statesman with power to enforce his opinions and arguments; it is the traveler's safety, and the business man's success. By the force of will the eagle mounts the heavens and tarries in the region of the clouds. By it the voracious wolf pursues the deer and destroys his prey. It is the power which moves mountains, builds railroads, clears away forests, digs tunnels, and makes a garden of a wild and arid waste.

Will is manifested in agreement of mind, as well as in disagreement. It presents itself in willingness as well as in stubbornness. It is the guard of our joy, and the restraint set upon our habits and passions in life. Will is often a source of abuse to the understanding and gives cause for sorrow, distress and regrets. It accommodates the loftiest pride of thought, and serves the lowest condition of being.

The principle of will is the responsible agent of Infinite Wisdom, and accomplishes the objects of Divine Desire through the inscrutable extremes of misery and happiness, of joy and sorrow, of light and darkness, of cold and heat, of white and black, of sweet and sour, of activity and rest, life and death.

The principle of will is the pivot upon which the universe revolves, and upon a knowledge of the movements and characteristics of this all-abounding element of nature as subdued by Omnipotent Wisdom, rests the confidence of spirits and angels in regard

K

to the future, and the safety of all things existing "in the house not made with hands suspended in the heavens."

CHAPTER XXII.

SPIRIT HEARING ESTABLISHED. IMPRISONED IN PSYCHOLOGY.   SUFFERING AND SUCCESS.

When I had finished the delivery of the article upon the subject of "The Principle of Will," which required several days at odd hours, I could see that mankind were living in utter ignorance in regard to the laws of mind, and I discovered—by trying to explain to others my own ideas concerning the matter—that it was almost, if not quite, impossible to so define the subject as to render it intelligible to them.   That I should be able to listen to the words and sentences of an unseen being in the presence of my family, and that they should hear nothing, and that I was at the same time in a position to be doubted—my individual honor being my chief safety in the confidence of others—was to me a very anamolous state of affairs, and equally a source of surprise, pleasure and wretchedness. My invisible guide permitted me to answer the *mental questions* of friends or strangers and this enabled me in a degree to dispose of various skeptical notions and objections which were offered as a set-off to my personal sincerity and honor.

I could now hear a spirit speak as easily as I could hear a mortal, but where they were, or how they were situated, was still as great a mystery as ever. The visions which I had enjoyed from childhood, and which became more definite, interesting and instructive as I advanced in years, indicated the existence of *life in the air* above and beyond the region of the clouds, but concerning this point my knowledge was as yet purely hypothetical, having its basis in inference, the laws of analogy, and the general tendencies of matter and mind as represented in nature.

I began to get thin in flesh as a result of my subjection to spirit-psychology, and the effect of the influence which was exerted over my entire mental organism began to be noticed by those around me, and I was counseled to desist from further pursuit of so dangerous an enterprise.

However willing I might have been to have complied with the kindly advice thus given, at the time to which reference is here made, it would have been impossible for me to have done so, owing to the fact of the *imprisonment* of my mental faculties,

so to speak, in the state of permanent trance, from
which to gain relief I had no remedy. I was depend-
ant upon my spirit magnetizer. His will was my
desire; and however much I might have objected to
his control—and I often did—the rule of superior
power was over me, and I yielded because it was
the operator's decision; *I being confined in a wish to
have it so.*

Thus after due consideration concerning my
own views and feelings, while I could but acknowledge my thankfulness for the wondrous gift of
clairaudience, although much of my experience was a
source of bickering annoyance, mortification and
distress. I resolved to say but little in regard to my
realizations, being convinced of the impropriety
of conversing with people upon a subject wholly
beyond the reach of ordinary understanding, and
which could be no source of direct benefit to individuals.

It was my determination, therefore, to put aside
all private explanations, and engage my pen in the
duty of writing a full statement in regard to what had
occurred to me as a psychologee under spirit control,
and present the same to the world in the plainest
and most practical language which I could command,
for the benefit of those who might desire to understand the more singular features connected with the
manifestations of mind, or who might become more
happy and better satisfied with life, through an
assurance that its continuance after the event of physical dissolution, could be no work of caprice, chance
or uncertainty; but was in truth a fact made per-

manent as a result of nature *in us*, and was an inheritance which, when once possessed, no mortal could either undo nor destroy.

The messages and articles which I had extemporaneously delivered—some of which contained many new and strange words, which were designed to be expressive of states, conditions, locations and places in the immortal realm—met with a heartfelt welcome from my Mother, Sister and family, and they were regarded as not only a source of hope, comfort and consolation, but as well an evidence of spirit kindness and condescension.

I had been privately counseled to retire to my studio, where I was advised to remain from three to five hours each day, for the purpose—as I have before intimated—of receiving aid as a student of literature. I accordingly took to the quiet of my library and became the psychologic pupil of a spirit diciplinarian in matters of letters, whose severity as a tutor was often quite as objectionable to my feelings, as it was undoubtedly beneficial in an intellectual point of view.

The mesmeric influence which was held over my mind was gradually augmented—imperceptably to my consciousness—and I soon lost the control of my mental faculties. My Brother and his associates in spirit life had nicely attuned their purposes to catch and *hold* me, in the clutch of enchantment, and I felt that they had too truly succeeded.*

* When a person is under the influence of spirit will—and I unhesitatingly say that no person of intelligence ever wholly escaped such influence—they are usually quite unconscious of it owing to a want of knowledge of the laws of mind. Only sensativeness and acquired habit enables the soul to realize every encroachment of mental power.

Day after day I continued writing, first upon one subject and then upon another, compounding or analyzing this sentence or paragraph, then shortening or lengthening some other, until I became a simple tool in the hands of an unseen operator who guided my thoughts, ideas and utterances with a force which I could not stay, and with a determination which I could not prevent.

I now began to reflect as well as I could concerning my own condition, for realizing that I was no longer master of my own mental *activities,* I began to have serious doubts as to the consequence of further permitting such influences to control me, and hence I struggled for relief.

I had become a complete instrument of use. A perfect machine of flesh and spirit. Had I been a believer in an orthodox devil I should certainly have felt that for some reason or other my interests in life had become associated with the machinations and devices of his *imperium* majesty, but as my Father had taught me that such a personage was but a fiction, and that the better interests of being were only to be secured through trials and sufferings, I concluded to bear my pains and difficulties with as much fortitude and forbearance as I could possibly command, and accept the derision of the spirit for the blessing which was thereby to be gained.

At the instigation of my magnetizer, with whom I was now in constant conversation, I was compelled to extemporize sentences, paragraphs, rondeaus, verses and original poems every moment of time during my wakeful hours.* The volumes of thought which entered my mind soon became oppressive and distressing. The whole theory of the origin, development and wondrous changes constantly occurring in nature—as comprehended by my spirit guide—was impressed upon my understanding. I was equally horrified and delighted. The extremes of goodness and wickedness, of joy and sorrow, of resolution and despair, of harmony and discord, of justice and misfortune, were all observed as a part of the Divine plan and as fundamental thereto. The extent of the creations of the universe as impressed upon my perceptions and thoughts, completely overwhelmed my

---

*Verses compounded of syllables in all manner of forms were enunciated in my mind and enforced in my utterance for days and weeks and months. This was said to be done in order to strengthen my memory, awaken thought, and facilitate ease in expression. The following is a specimen of the verses which I repeated, sometimes with wondrous rapidity for twelve hours together:

> Mar—tol A—ni Le—ne—won,
> E—mo Wan—ti Ax—a—lon;
> Bantz—e A—na Mex—o—no,
> In—tor Al—vi Ba—na—yo.

> A—mon I—mon O—mon In,
> Le—vor Al—ti Ma—ni—win;
> Ken—e—ke Kon—e—ko A—fal—so,
> Ips—a—von Ar—la—von Ma—na—yo.

The "spell of the spirit" in which I delivered these singular verses would be regarded as demoniacal, no doubt, by many persons, and by giving expression to them openly any individual would be considered insane. I regret exceedingly that I am unable to give a more perfect representation of this matter, spirits object to it and refuse to give me aid, obstructing my memory by psychologic processes whenever I attempt to write upon the subject—or otherwise I would give the details of an experience so wondrous, so exalting, yet at times so terrible, as an evidence of heartless wisdom, of God-like greatness of mind beyond the earth, that all tampering with the "immortals" would cease forever. The simplicity of our knowledge is destroyed in the "world beyond." The law of *amplification in mystery* as made manifest in spirit demonstrations and communion, hides from our perception that unmeasured intelligence which the "invisibles" possess.

consciousness and the peace of my soul, and I begged to be released from realizations so painful, from sights so harassing and extraordinary; but all to no effect. I was deeply entranced in mind. My ideas were *fomented*. My will was not my own. I was taken from my writing and directed to wander out in the fields. I sat down in this place and that place all alone, listening to and repeating volumes of new and singular sentiments, which flowed into my mind like the current of a river. I could not prevent their introduction by any means at my command. My mind was being played upon like a piano. At times my consciousness was wholly lost. I began to be frightened, terrorized, and I cursed with a fearful utterance.

At the pleasure of my operator—all unseen—yet now much against my own judgment—my will being no longer my own to control—I stood for hours in an old back shed which ajoined the barn near my dwelling and gave expression to the thoughts and words—marvelously compounded—which descended into my mind with great power and rapidity. Twice during ten days, while I was in the deepest abnormal condition to which I attained, my tongue and mental faculties were held so perfectly within the control of my magnetizer, that any language forced upon my sensibilities was uttered with the greatest freedom.* In this condition, and while compelled to weep like a child, I spoke the most beautiful and flowing tongue known to the spirit *Sivihs*† of the *In-te-un* realm. I can never forget

*This state of mind was *missioned* in the Messiah.
†Spirits of great age and wondrous wisdom.

the sweet accent of that inimitable monosyllabic language, and I could only give expression to it in my tears.

After I had been thus beset by spirit influence for many days and weeks, and notwithstanding there was much of interest in my experience, I found my distresses greater than I could bear, and in anxiety for my own safety, I said to my guardian:

"For God sake give me peace, or otherwise destroy me if you will."

I was really more frightened than hurt, for being mostly unacquainted with the laws of mind, at least in a practical sense, I supposed that if I too long permitted this mesmeric control of my spirit, it might result in permanent personal injury if not death. But my counsels were ever forthcoming. My Brother advised me to bear my pains with patience, adding:

"You will soon be released from your trials. Dont worry, neither fear."

I had become sick of promises. My caution had been aroused, and I vowed that I would not submit to such treatment. When compelled to yield to psychologic power I stamped my foot, clutched my teeth, and tore my hair in my willful resistance. I made a desperate struggle to regain my normal condition of mind; but all to no effect. I soon discovered that to wrestle with the angels* was an

---

*The wrestling of Jacob with the angel at Peniel, as recorded in the thirty-second chapter of Genesis, is no longer a subject to be misunderstood, when the influence of psychology as exercised by spirits is properly comprehended. It is very evident, judging from the scriptural record, that not only Jacob the

unhallowed undertaking, and I concluded to beg my
way out if possible. In this I met with but indifferent success. Indeed I began to realize that silence
and submission were the better part of valor, and so
I wept in my misery.

Day after day my trance deepened. I was
made to weep, talk, sing, laugh and sigh. My
tongue was actually moved by the descending will-
force of my operator, and my thoughts were like a
flowing river, continuous, incessant and distressing.*
My senses were wondrously acute and active, and
were played upon in a thousand different ways.
These influences all came through the *top of my head.*
So sensitive had I become that I could feel the will-
power of my spirit guide, passing downward through
my skin and skull into the corrugated cell-substance
of my brain, where it seemed to grasp by an
astringent force the nerve-connections with every
function of my body. In this I felt all the sensations
—intensified—natural to my own consciousness, and
I learned something of that righteous law or
method of *silent, heavenly counsel in the earth,*† which
is conceeded by spirits and angels. The whole
arcanum of the spiritual philosophy was revealed to
my comprehension. I could see its faults and its

Egyptian, but likewise Daniel the Mede, Ezekiel, and St. John the Revelator
were held as subjects of spirit-psychology for a purpose wisely appointed in the
interest of human life. The time is coming, however, when it will be understood that a seer is only a seer; and is as well a prophet in *mistakes* as in the
truthfulness of foreknowledge.

*The effect of this pressure upon the mind is to enlarge the capacity
of thought, and aid in disciplining ideas.

†The law of "angel ministration."

blessings. The production of "physical phenomena and mediumship," I soon learned were the result of "Wise Design" on the part of the "immortals." The ultimate object of spirit communion was more considered than *present* mortal joy and satisfaction. I was delighted with the many impressions which I received concerning nature. This was my greatest source of happiness, and in my reflections upon this subject I felt the weight of a sense of knowledge which rendered impotent every human thought.

I now began to feel sad, sorrowful and subdued, and I resolved that I would endure with patience and fortitude the pangs and pains which were heaped upon me; although I could not forbear from complaint when overdosed with mental activity, or when my mind was strained by inordinate exercise as a result of a propelling power of spirit will.

After having remained in this condition for many weeks, and after having endured, as I thought, untold misery, my guide who was in constant conversational communion with me — the clairaudience of my mind having been fully established—very unexpectedly remarked :

"We shall be obliged to induce a much deeper state of trance than you have yet experienced, my Brother, in order to facilitate your educational progress and aid you to a better knowledge concerning "spiritual things," and I hope you may yield to the discipline thus conferred with freedom and composure."

This information was everything but a comfort to my already wounded feelings, and with a sigh, I said:

"Oh dear, what was I about when I asked spirits to come and converse with me."

Perceiving my thoughts and knowing that I suffered deeply, my Brother remarked:

"You need not fear; we will not harm you. You have requested me to aid you. It is not my purpose to refuse. Clairvoyance is not attained without difficulty. Success in your case is a mere matter of procrastination.* Our psychologic processes may be a cause of annoyance to your peace, but give yourself no distress. I will endeavor to satisfy your anxiety by just and reasonable explanations."

These words coming opportunely, caused my heart to rejoice, and although it was no source of pleasure to be held in the embrace of mesmeric control my Brother's timely advice was never lost, but in the end alone enabled me to pass all disagreeableness and mental inquietude with safety, if not with satisfaction.

For many days I became entranced as often as five times in twenty-four hours and although my feelings were many times greatly harrowed up, and painful to endure, I preferred not to speak of them, from the fact that it was a cause of distress to my family, and I had already been informed that the

*Why this word should have been used I do not know.

spirits would make me insane if I continued to
solicit their help.

Thus I kept my own counsel, and giving no
heed to the insinuations of those around me, I gradually but surely became the recipient of the most
estatic visions in clairvoyance. The entire philosophy
of the production of sensitive dreams and mental
impressions was explained to my comprehension.
Various grand and startling scenes were enstamped
upon the latent elements of consciousness in my soul.
The wonders of life, as represented among the *Livleun*
hosts who dwell in the realm of elysian grandeur on
the far heights of our enveloping atmosphere, and
their relationship to earthly races, nations and
populations, were mapped in the beautiful pictures
which were cast upon my inner sight in stereoscopic
perfection.

Rising from the earth during periods of entrancement, my spirit seemed to wander in freedom for
hundreds of miles through aereal stratums, as the
freed spirit is supposed to in its unseen abode
of silent happiness. The untold and inexpressible
grandeur pertaining to the appearance of other
worlds, their people, their vegetable and animal
productions, their oceans, rivers and mountains, their
phenomenal aspects and visible characteristics; all
these became distinctly impressed—through the
natural channels of the senses—upon the consciousness of my mind, and my delight was unbounded.

The pains and penalties connected with the
enforced mesmeric process of education through
which I had passed, gradually subsided, and although

I had many times begged to be released from psychologic influence, I still felt that the knowledge which I had gained was worth more to me than all the riches of the earth, and I wept in thankfulness when 1 contemplated the happiness which it was mine to experience in view of the permission which I enjoyed of conferring with the deceased member of my Father's household, and of gaining an insight into the nature of that future life which all mankind so sincerely yearn to possess.

My spirit guide had taught me much concerning the process of organizing and compounding words, sentences and paragraphs; had unfolded to my comprehension the principles involved in the origin of language, directing my attention to an exposition of the methods employed by spirits in analyzing, dissecting and sundering authorities in literature, and making a complete revelation of the insecurity of all worded productions, and the imperfection of oral speech.

One day as I was walking in the open field, having been out upon my farm, looking after some local interest, I experienced a reception of the flowing elements of sympathy from my spirit Father's mind, and stopping for a moment, I listened while he uttered these words: *"Go—to—the—house—my son,—I—have—something—of—moment—to—tell—you."*

Obeying his command I directed my footsteps toward home, when retiring to the little room which I usually occupied in writing, and taking my pen in hand I wrote, at his request, the following brief message which was delivered to my keeping as a matter of needful counsel:

"Only yesterday I came to speak with you, but finding you engaged, I withdrew without affecting the object of my solicitude. I desire, my son, that you should follow such directions in regard to your habits of life as we may from time to time see fit to advice. We shall recommend to you the adoption of a most thorough system of physical training and mental discipline. Your clothing must be warm and comfortable, your food selected. If you will be obedient to your Brother's suggestions he will aid you in restraining your appetites and guiding you to better methods of living, that you may have more perfect health and consequently greater comfort. As spirits are reticent of a disclosure of the essential characteristics pertaining to their condition of being, you should not be too exacting in your demands upon our regard, for the best interests of earth and heaven require that we should make no hasty disclosures."*

My Father having thus spoken with me simply remarked:

"Be blessed, my son!" And I heard him no more.

At the time to which reference is here made or just previous my bodily weight was one hundred and eighty-one pounds. I had often noticed and frequently remarked to those around me, that as I

*My Father had been in spirit life but eighteen months when this message was given.

advanced in years I amassed physical substance and
more closely resembled my Father who was in old
age a very corpulent man*—unfortunately a minister—and that if I continued to grow fleshy, I
should one day become his equal in bodily proportions, which was really not a very agreeable thing
to contemplate; but following the timely admonitions
of my Brother, as given subsequently to the inter-
view which I had with my Father, I began to
observe a decided falling off in the amount of my flesh,
and it was not more than three months before I had
become much emaciated.   I grew weak and feeble, was
nervous and irritable, and trembled upon the least
exertion, until slowly, but surely, I was reduced to
the, to me, extremely meager weight of one hundred
and thirty-nine pounds or in other words, I sustained
an absolute reduction of forty-two pounds from the
material constituents of my mortal form.†

My neighbors noticing the extraordinary poverty
of my appearance, now began to inquire concerning
my health, saying:

"You must have been quite sick, Mr. Wright."
"Why, how pale and thin you look." "Have you
been long confined to the house?" "I am sorry to
see you looking so poorly." "I hope you will soon

*His weight was 225 pounds.

†The author does n t believe that history furnishes a parallel instance
of physical emaciation as produced by the mesmeric influence of spirits, and he
is quite as certain that through the exercise of the same power, slow, but sure,
starvation could be produced.   The reader may have a laugh at my expense,
if he feels so inclined for I did surely quarrel with my spirit Brother on account
of fasting so long.   Indeed, I am disposed to think that I really outdone Daniel
the Hebrew prophet, in starvation processes by many a month.

be better." With many similar expressions of surprise and sympathy.

Thus I was daily reminded of my condition by my family and others, until I appealed to my spirit magnetizer with words of severe animadversion, to withdraw his influence from the control of my mental faculties, and especially that *of alimentiveness* —desire for food—which had been the cause of the depletion of the chemical constituents of my body, and consequently of the wan and frail appearance which I presented.

In a few weeks I began to recuperate. The wondrous change which I had experienced, while it had been a cause of great displeasure as well as suffering to myself, was at the same time productive of much improvement in the condition of my mind. My thoughts were more clearly defined and active, and subjects which had previously cost me a vast amount of reflection without satisfactory result, were no longer difficult of solution. Sights and scenes more gorgeous and beautiful than the imagination is capable of picturing, rose before my trance awakened senses during sleep, causing me to realize feelings of excessive delight and happiness. Other scenes more loathsome and disgusting than all our conceptions of distress, degradation or satanic horror were impressed upon my sense of vision, until the sight became sickening and painful to witness.

It soon became my delight to induce mental illumination. Whenever my condition admitted of a propriety in so doing I could lie down upon my couch or bed, and, soliciting aid from above, would

soon feel a drowsyness stealing over my conscious
thoughts, accompanied by a dizzy sensation which
hovered over my soul until my mind was lost to all
outward realizations. In this state of somnambulic
sleep, and by mesmeric processes gently employed
and only known to spirits, my mental faculties
would be gradually aroused to activity, and my perception and consciousness were thus rendered abnormally vivid and sensitive in the extreme. In this
clairvoyant light of mental experience, in which I
often remained for hours, and in which I was
cautiously held by the will-force of my invisible
guide, I contemplated the scenes addressed to my
understanding or realized every natural ability to
observe and reflect, which comes within the province
of the organic functions of the mind. In this condition—through super-induced action of the senses—
I beheld and conversed with spirits; I felt every
emotion of joy, sorrow, exaltation and humility.
Thoughts as brilliant as lightning, as sweet and
agreeable as loveliness, or as dark, oppressive and
horrifying as the chains of hades, brooded over my
soul's inner consciousness. Sweet and gentle music
resounded upon my ear, or discordant notes worried
my sense of joy and disturbed my admiration for
the delightful harmony expressed in accordant sounds.

I could now see that I was gradually returning
to my former condition of mind, with the added
glorious privilege of *hearing* and *seeing* in the spirit,
whenever it might be deemed wise or beneficial,
during the few remaining years of my earthly life.

Thus I had suffered the pains and anxieties, the

doubts, trials and misgivings, consequent upon becoming the subject of an overmastering psychologic
power; and even as this influence came upon me
almost imperceptably, slowly but surely binding my
mental faculties in subdued, subordinate action, as
was optional with the wisdom of my spirit operator,
so as gradually—after about two years—was I
released from nearly every unpleasant *imposed*
influence, sensation and emotion, and my mind was
no longer held in abeyance of another's desires and
will.   As I regained my freedom from the state
of *mental imprisonment* which I had so long endured,
I retained all the memories which were developed as
a result of my abnormal visions, conversations,
journeyings and contemplations "in the spirit," AND I
WAS COMPARATIVELY FREE.

Religio-Philosophical

PUBLISHING HOUSE

JNO. C. BUNDY, *Secretary.*   S. S. JONES, *Proprietor.*

Chicago, Illinois.

This House, though it met with the total destruction of its entire Stock and Machinery in the "Great Fire," never ceased business for a day, and with greatly increased facilities continues to publish and deal in **Liberal and Reformatory Books** tending to the elucidation of the *Philosophy of Life*, Spiritualism, &c.

It also publishes the

Religio-Philosophical Journal,

a large eight page weekly Newspaper, devoted to the promulgation of *Spiritualism*, in the highest sense of the phrase. The Journal should be in the hands of every person seeking truth. Sample copies sent *Free* on application. In the Journal will be found a very complete and valuable list of all books published or for sale by this House.

☞ *Address as above.*

CONFUCIUS,

HIS

MORAL AXIOMS & TEACHINGS

Eight thousand copies sold.

A CORRECT LIKENESS OF

The Great Philosopher,

The most worthy code of Moral Precepts in

the English Language,

Bound in Paper Covers, 25 Cts., in Cloth, 50 Cts.

Orders Solicited.

ADDRESS,

M. R. K. WRIGHT,

Middleville, Barry Co., Mich.

www.ingramcontent.com/pod-product-compliance
Lightning Source LLC
Chambersburg PA
CBHW030357270326
41926CB00009B/1142